"It is a landmark"
~ Dr. Susan and Dr. Bob Carlson

Located at the top of a hill on a remote island near Sitka, Alaska, the Carlson's new relaxation retreat is already well known to Pacific coast fishermen.

"They use it as a landmark", laughs Dr. Susan Carlson of the get-away home she and her husband, Dr. Bob Carlson, recently finished building.

The isolated location posed a number of challenges, which the Carlsons were well aware of when they decided to look for a company that could help them build it. With no roads, no outside communication, and no electricity, it was certainly not a conventional type of arrangement—nor was the design of the home they wanted.

"We were looking for something that would fit in with the environment," she explains.

The interest and cooperation they got from their Linwood sales representative impressed them enough to trust him and the rest of his crew to take on the challenge. And, as Dr. Carlson says, they're glad they did.

"It could have been a disaster if everything that was supposed to be sent up wasn't included," says Dr. Carlson, recalling how the materials were sent from British Columbia to Sitka, then transported by helicopter. "But it was all there."

They were impressed with the company's dedication to the project after the delivery. "It wasn't just a drop-it-off and forget about the Carlsons," she says. "We could call them any time we wanted to, and they were very helpful to us throughout the whole process." Their contractor was appreciative of the follow-up as well.

see page 48

A Letter from the Publisher

Finally, the right book for the right time.

Garlinghouse and Linwood Homes are pleased to announce the creation of the Live Your Dream Collection in this title, Timber Dream Homes. In this book, we are proud to offer you:

• A broad selection of popular designs with highly desirable features, created by the top designers in the country.
• The opportunity to build a house with top quality building materials, not available at your local lumberyard.
• The ability to have these high quality building materials delivered right to your construction site.
• The option to have an experienced construction crew build your home at reasonable prices.

Experience you can trust:

For over 90 years, Garlinghouse has helped build the American dream. Almost one million customers have purchased our blueprints. Our success is based upon our reputation to provide the right designs for the right time. Garlinghouse markets home designs from fifty of the top designers in the country. Approximately thirty of these designers have received awards in recognition of their excellence. As a result, Garlinghouse is one of the nation's top home plan providers.

For over 30 years, Linwood Homes has provided complete home construction packages for thousands of customers across the country and around the world. These packages are customized to suit each client's specific needs and the materials are all supported by a full warranty. Linwood has a high commitment to quality and service. Their outstanding reputation is the reason why Garlinghouse has teamed up with Linwood, to provide you with this unique designer series of home packages.

A partnership that makes sense for you:

Garlinghouse has the designs to meet your needs. Linwood Homes has the sales staff, draftsmen, technical knowledge and experience to help you use these designs to plan and then build your custom home with quality building materials.

Please take the time to enjoy this book:

There are well over one hundred spectacular photos in full color, with multiple plan illustrations, to help you select your home. Also, our editors have provided several pages of planning information to increase your comfort level with making such an important decision in your life.

We look forward to helping you Live Your Dream. From us to you,

James D. McNair III
Chief Executive Officer-Garlinghouse Company

the
Garlinghouse
company

HELPING TO BUILD DREAMS
SINCE 1907

Libarary of Congress No.: 00-136081
ISBN: 0-938708-98-8
Cover Photography supplied by Linwood Homes

From our family to yours...

the Garlinghouse company

HELPING TO BUILD DREAMS
SINCE 1907

Chief Executive Officer/Publisher James D. McNair, III, **Chief Operating Officer/Editor-in-Chief** Bradford J. Kidney, **Home Plan Coordinator** Debbie Cochran, **Operations Manager** Susan Barile, **Marketing Assistant** Louise Ryan, **Financial Controller** Doug DiMora, **Personnel Assistant** Elizabeth Unikewicz, **Senior Accounting Assistant** Angela West, **Editor** Steve Culpepper, **Director of Operations** Wade Schmelter, **Assistant Design Director** Michael Rinaldi, **Design Staff** Don Miner, Bruce Newman, **Art Production Staff** Debra Novitch, Andrew Russell, Reagan Guerrera **Telesales Manager** Frank Shekosky, **Telesales Staff** Robert Rogala, Lisa Barnes, Carol Patenaude, Jeanne Willett, Anne Hawkins, Mary Jane Forsythe, **Receptionist** Barbara Neal, **Senior Programmer** Jason Cyr, **Plans Fulfillment Manager** Wayne Green, **Fulfillment Assistant** Audrey Sutton

LINWOOD *custom homes*

President & Chief Executive Officer Bill Mascott, **Vice President** Yvonne Darcel, **Regional Managers** Carl Hall, Craig McFarlane, Tom Woods, **Export Sales Manager** Brad Grindler, **Area Manager** Tom Abbott, **Customer Service & Transportation Manager** Denise Seder, **Communications** Aimee Parkin, **Marketing** Karen Swantje, **Drafting & Design Manager** Daryl Martens, **Assistant Drafting Manager** Barry Hryciw, Mike Van Dop, **Design Team** Nick George, Ron Linden, Herre Negenman, Kevin Okano, Grady Ott, Mike Van Dop, Tony Walker, **Senior Estimators** Stewart Adams, Ted Blackall, Mark MacDonald, Perry Schebel, Barry Spence, **Purchasing** Roy Gattinger, Dylan Read, **Accounting & Administration** Pat Graham, Laurie Jordan, Cindy McConnell, **Shipping Manager** Randy Langton, **Shipping Team** Tim Herder, Dean St. John, David Watkins, **Trucking** Dino Garofano, Larry Lupien, **Sawmill Manager** Tim Garofano, **Head Sawyer** Leo Lalonde, **Edgerman/Leadhand Sawmill** Brad Massender, **Senior Planerman** Hans Bert, **Quality Control** Al Robinson **Millwrights** Barry Johnson, Sam Ota, Gail Akin, **Sawmill Team** Mike Boyles, Fred Clark, Brian Geldart, Raymond Marsh, Greg Netzlaw, Simon Simonsen, Darrin Stuppard, **Sawmill Team** Jake Bergen, David Budzak, Jerry Geldart, Helmut Starch **And the entire Linwood Sales Network**

Graphic Design Terrain Design Inc.

www.linwoodhomes.com

About Linwood Homes

Since 1968, Linwood Custom Homes has been making dreams come true. Our commitment to unsurpassed selection, quality and service has brought many of our customers back to build a second and third Linwood home. No wonder we are one of the fastest growing home suppliers in North America today.

With Linwood Homes, you not only choose your house design—you can customize it, order all the quality materials to create it, and have all those components shipped anywhere in the world. You can even locate the closest Linwood recommended builder to construct it for you. Plus, you'll have one of the strongest warranty programs in the industry backing you up, every step of the way.

In this outstanding new book you will find over 80 distinctive designer home plans for inspiration. Our experienced design team can fully modify any of these plans to create your unique home. Or you can create a completely new customized floor plan and exterior from your imagination. Whatever your needs, our experts can turn your vision into an exclusive, one-of-a-kind home.

Why buy only a plan, when with Linwood Homes, you can have the whole custom package!

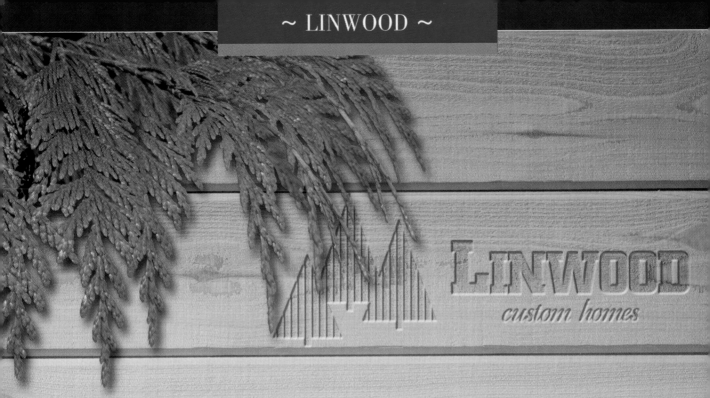

The Linwood Advantage

Custom Design

You can customize any of our over 150 stock plans featured in our two full color Plan Books, to accommodate your own unique lifestyle needs.

Or, if you already have a home plan fully designed or even a daydream sketch in your head, our experienced design and building experts can take your ideas and produce your beautiful home. Our team uses the latest computer technology to efficiently and professionally create detailed blueprints that your builder can depend on.

Whether your heart's desire is a Victorian farmhouse, a Log home, a Cape Cod bungalow, or a Cedar contemporary—the Linwood team can deliver.

You can build on Linwood's decades of home design expertise at no extra cost!

High Quality Construction Materials

All Linwood cedar siding and interior cedar components are made with Western Red Cedar— one of the finest building materials in the world. It's naturally durable, dimensionally stable, and exceptionally versatile to work with. Above all— it's beautiful!

We operate our own sawmill in order to control and maintain the quality of all our cedar components, from the log all the way to the finished product.

All Linwood framing lumber is certified by the North American Lumber Grading Association, and acknowledged as the best available.

All our other construction materials are supplied by major brand-name manufacturers and certified to national home building standard specifications. These include architectural laminated beams, plywood, windows, doors and roofing material. Plus, we've searched North America to bring you a wide selection of specialty items like Victorian gingerbread and Georgian shutters. We put our buying power to work for you to obtain superior products at an advantageous price.

Full Warranty Program

Linwood has a full structural warranty on all home packages good for ten years. Our warranty is in turn supported by the individual warranties of all our suppliers. This powerful combination provides our customers with one of the strongest warranty programs available in the industry today.

World Wide Shipping Expertise

We have built homes all over the world from the U.S. to Germany to Japan. We specialize in hard to reach destinations where it is imperative that everything needed for construction is included in the package. Our home packages have been delivered to building sites by truck, container, barge and even helicopter. You can depend on Linwood to deliver!

Construction Support

We offer a variety of levels of construction support—everything from detailed construction blueprints and manuals, to a recommended network of experienced builders. As an additional option, we even panelize wall units for rapid and easy assembly.

Our Sales & Design Consultants can provide assistance in selecting contractors, receiving and evaluating quotes, obtaining planning permits, and monitoring on-site job performance by the selected sub-trades. We also have a toll-free hotline number to answer construction questions, plus construction experts who can provide detailed instruction on the fastest and most efficient method of assembling one of our homes.

What's in a Package?

With Linwood, you are purchasing a home package. This package includes the following:

- Construction blueprints
- Framing lumber and plywood to build walls and floors
- Siding in a wide variety of materials, styles, colors and finishes
- Customized windows and skylights
- An extensive selection of exterior doors
- Roofing materials
- House wrap
- Rust-proof nails

These options are also available:

- Sunrooms and solariums
- Decking and railing
- Interior doors in many styles
- Architectural detailing—shutters, gingerbread etc.
- Drywall and insulation

Your Linwood Homes package will have all the components you need to complete your home to "lock-up stage". This means that you can then complete your interior finishing, electrical and plumbing in a fully weatherproof environment at your own pace. Individual considerations, needs and styles vary considerably for interior finishing. Consult your Linwood Representative for more details.

From the Woods to the Sawmill

Linwood Homes has secured its own timber licenses through programs operated by the Ministry of Forests in British Columbia, Canada. All Linwood logs are professionally harvested by contractors who understand their future is dependent on looking after the forests. The Linwood logging operations not only include harvesting the timber, but also reforesting the land and maintaining the seedlings so they survive to maturity. No logs are harvested from environmentally sensitive areas.

This controlled harvesting allows for a consistent supply of high quality timber, which is utilized in all Linwood home packages. This wood is of a uniformly high standard and is widely agreed to be the best available in the world marketplace today.

From the Sawmill...

All cedar products are manufactured by Linwood at its own sawmill, in order to control and maintain the outstanding quality of our wood components.

We also manufacture a wide range of components with customized patterns, to meet higher performance standards than commonly available in the market. We can even profile siding on a custom basis, creating a unique look just for you.

...To You

Linwood Homes ships worldwide, from New York to Frankfurt to Osaka. Our home packages are delivered to building sites by truck, container, barge and helicopter. From the remotest island to the busiest metropolis, we can deliver your dream home.

Making a House a Home

A house is walls, floors, doors, windows and a roof. A home is a haven—a place that provides its owners with a warm welcome, sanctuary, and a sense of pride. Turning a house into a home requires thoughtful planning to ensure all your needs are taken care of.

When choosing and designing your home, there are some fundamental questions to ask yourself:

- *How do you move through your surroundings during the day?*
- *What would be a logical flow from room to room, for your daily routines?*
- *Do you spend a lot of time in a formal living room or dining room, or would these traditional spaces be better utilized as a media room, home office, or hobby space?*
- *Do you like to entertain casually or formally, big groups or small?*
- *Where do you like to eat? Read? Listen to music? Watch TV?*
- *Have you made room for private space?*
- *Have you ensured plenty of room for your favorite activitie?*

Once you have determined your lifestyle needs, then you can begin the wonderful process of creating your exclusive home. There are many design features that turn an ordinary plan into an original masterpiece. Signature windows showcase not only the exterior of your home, but they also highlight your views from the interior. Well-placed windows maximize the natural light, bringing a spacious, soft glow to every room. Great Rooms, with cathedral ceilings and distinctive windows, become the heart of your home.

Many people use a formal living room or dining room only on rare occasions, so there is more call for open floor plans, combining kitchen, dining, and entertaining areas into one magnificent, multi-use space. Porches, decks and patios extend your living quarters during good weather, and add a visual welcome to the exterior design all year around.

Luxury in private spaces like bedrooms, ensuites and studies are a way to create "a room of your own" when you need time to relax and reflect. Keep in mind your art and collections, the things that you love, so you can design special areas to show them off.

When it comes time to decorate your new home, there are many tricks that professional designers use to make distinguishing statements. If you like color, don't be afraid to use it! Choose colors you are drawn to, colors you like wearing, colors that inspire you to smile. Homes have personality, humor, and style that reflect their owners. Use dimmer switches with your lighting so you can adjust the light with the phases of the day, the weather, and moods.

Alcoves and built-in benches, cabinets and bookshelves are timeless additions that can be customized to create one-of-a-kind rooms. Fireplaces add a warm ambience in any room, including master bedrooms and kitchens.

The floorings you choose have a big impact on the overall impression of each room, they can add

feelings of coziness, elegance, or drama. Linwood's Interiors division can certainly assist you with design and selection of these products and more to create at truly distinctive home. See pages 130 and 131 for further details.

Above all, remember that this house is your home. It's a wood and glass reality borne out of your desire to create the perfect place to hang your hat.

Make it unique!

Denise Seder
John Collins ~ Renaissance Design

The Live Your Dream Collection

The following pages showcase over 80 distinctive designer homes. There are a wide variety of styles and sizes, and every plan can be customized by our design experts to meet your individual needs.

This specially selected collection of homes share some characteristics that we feel make them particularly delightful:

- Outstanding interior design
- Great Rooms
- Open floor plans for entertaining
- Use of distinctive windows and natural light
- Cathedral ceilings
- Luxurious master suites
- Gourmet kitchens
- Striking exteriors
- Porches & decks
- Architectural details
- The richness of natural wood

We are pleased to bring this unique collection to you for the first time. Contact us to start turning your new dream home into reality.

HELPING TO BUILD DREAMS SINCE 1907

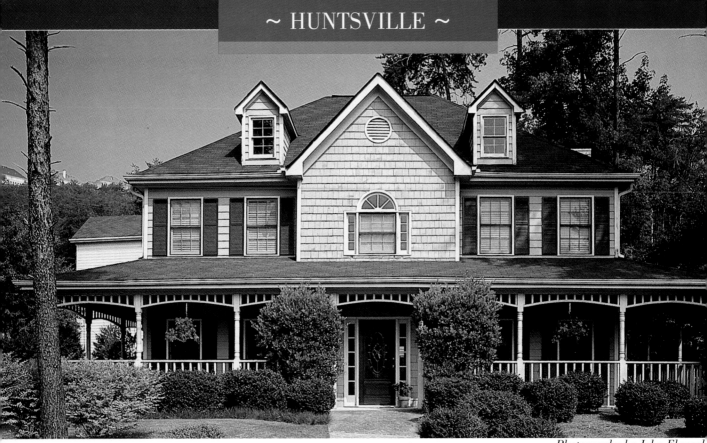

Photography by John Ehrencl

2,588 sq. ft

- This charming Southern-style four bedroom home features many special extras, including a separate breakfast room, large bonus room upstairs and a luxurious master suite.

- Large family room offers a cozy fireplace and a view of the patio or deck.

- Formal cross-hall living and dining rooms look out on to the wrap-around veranda.

FIRST FLOOR

DBL. GARAGE
22'-8" X 21'-2"

WH

BREAKFAST
14'-10" X 10'-4"

STOR.

DECK OR PATIO
21'-8" X 12'-0"

W D

REF.

FAMILY ROOM
21'-4" X 13'-6"

KITCHEN
13'-0 X 11'-0"

OVEN

PANT. ALT STAIRS
TO BSMT.

DINING ROOM
13'-0" X 11'-6"

LIVING ROOM
15'-6" X 11'-6"

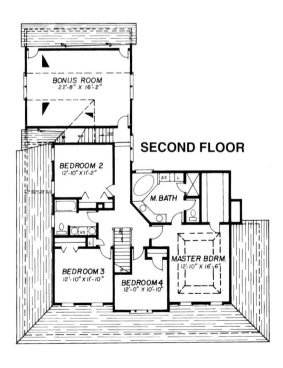

BONUS ROOM
22'-8" X 16'-2"

SECOND FLOOR

BEDROOM 2
12'-10" X 11'-2"

KS L

M. BATH

KS

BEDROOM 3
12'-10" X 11'-10"

BEDROOM 4
12'-0" X 10'-10"

MASTER BDRM.
12'-10" X 16'-6"

2,525 sq. ft

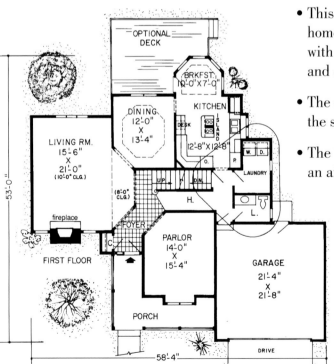

- This interesting and well-designed three bedroom home features a large front-facing master bedroom with a box-bay window, his and hers walk-in closets and ensuite.

- The dining room has a octagonal recessed ceiling and the sunny breakfast room has a window on every wall.

- The high ceiling in the spacious living room ensures an airy atmosphere.

©2000 ROGER WADE

1,768 sq. ft.

- Relax in the warm, rustic interior of this peaceful weekend retreat. The distinct focal point of this one-room log cabin is the window-flanked fireplace in the living room. Upstairs, the cozy loft makes a perfect bedroom.

- A complete kitchen and one full bath make this design a fully functional home. The real outdoor lover will appreciate a woodland setting from the outdoor living space of the covered porch. Perfect as a vacation home or a quaint weekend getaway.

UPPER FLOOR

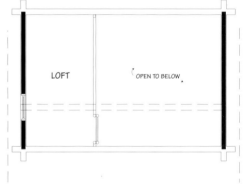

LOFT   OPEN TO BELOW

MAIN FLOOR

BATH

LIVING ROOM

KITCHEN

COVERED PORCH

1,860 sq. ft.

- Broad, projecting roof lines distinguish the design of this gorgeous three bedroom home. Both stone and a wide profile cedar siding have been used to create a striking exterior effect.

- The master bedroom, with corner-tub ensuite and adjacent loft, is located on the private second level.

- The huge country kitchen, separate dining area, vaulted living room with prow front, and wraparound sundeck ensure comfortable living on the main level.

MAIN FLOOR

DOUBLE GARAGE
24'-0"x24'-0"

BEDROOM
12'-0"x12'-0"

UTILITY   ENTRY

KITCHEN
12'-8"x10'-6"

BEDROOM
12'-0"x12'-0"

UP

BATH

DINING ROOM
15'-6"x12'-0"

DN

LIVING ROOM
20'-0"x11'-6"

SUNDECK

UPPER FLOOR

MASTER
BEDROOM
12'-0"x15'-6"

ENSUITE

LOFT
14'-0"x12'-0"

DN

OPEN TO BELOW

Photography by Beth Singer

1,487 sq. ft.

- This compact contemporary three-bedroom home has a large deck which provides extra living space and brings in the outdoors.

- One of the bedrooms on the second floor features a deck, and the second floor landing balcony overlooks the living room.

- The versatility of the basic design is shown in the above photograph by the addition of a two-car garage and a large family room

FIRST FLOOR

SECOND FLOOR

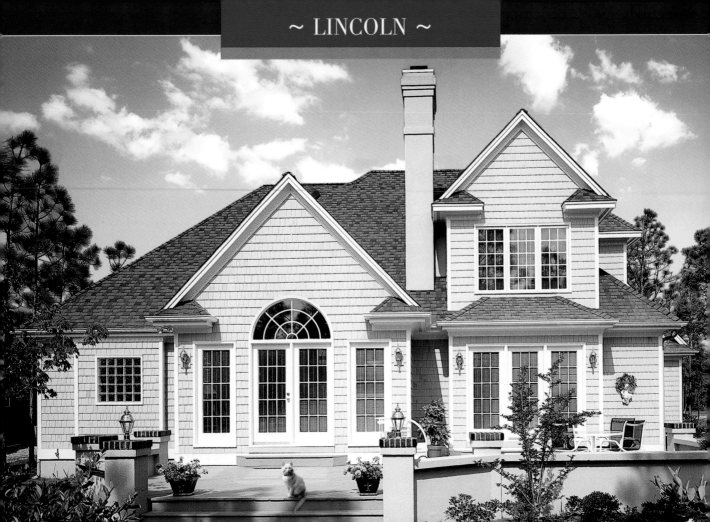

Photography by Jon Riley, Riley & Riley Photograp

1,861 sq. ft

- This delightful 3-bedroom home is filled with sunshine and light through the many distinctive windows. These include an arched palladian window in the great room.

- Interior columns add elegance while visually dividing the foyer from the dining room and the great room from the kitchen.

- The master suite, secluded on the first floor, features his and her walk-in closets as well as a garden tub with a skylight.

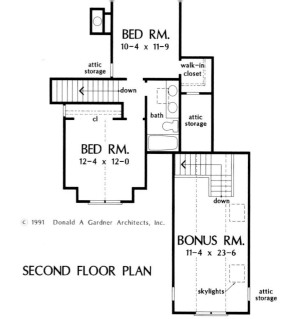

BED RM.
10-4 x 11-9

attic
storage

walk-in
closet

down

cl

bath

attic
storage

BED RM.
12-4 x 12-0

down

SECOND FLOOR PLAN

BONUS RM.
11-4 x 23-6

skylights

attic
storage

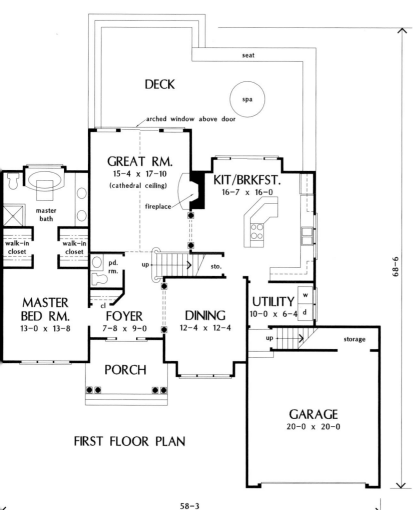

seat

DECK

spa

arched window above door

GREAT RM.
15-4 x 17-10
(cathedral ceiling)

KIT/BRKFST.
16-7 x 16-0

fireplace

master
bath

walk-in
closet

walk-in
closet

up

sto.

pd.
rm.

cl

**MASTER
BED RM.**
13-0 x 13-8

FOYER
7-8 x 9-0

DINING
12-4 x 12-4

UTILITY
10-0 x 6-4

w
d

up

storage

PORCH

68-9

FIRST FLOOR PLAN

GARAGE
20-0 x 20-0

58-3

1,932 sq. ft

- A popular design, this distinctive four bedroom home features the exceptional use of glass and the privacy of a second-level master bedroom with walk-in closet and full ensuite.

- Amenities on the main level include the vaulted living room, open-plan dining area, and a delightfully large country kitchen.

- Three bedrooms, another full bath, and the utility/mudroom complete this superb floor plan.

MAIN FLOOR

UPPER FLOOR

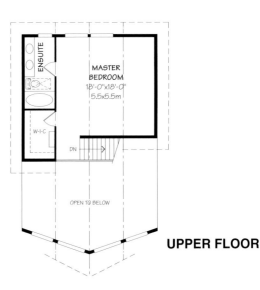

Photography by supplied by Ahmann Design

3,113 sq. ft.

- An appealing archway leads into the living room from a vaulted-ceiling entry hall. A see-through fireplace divides the living room and family room in this picturesque four bedroom home.

- The large kitchen area with island and walk-in pantry, incorporates a cathedral ceiling in the nook/sun room, which in turn leads to an attractive screened porch.

- The spacious main floor master suite includes a corner spa tub, his and hers vanity, separate shower stall and large walk-in closet.

SECOND FLOOR

FIRST FLOOR

DINING ROOM
19'-0"x12'-0"

LAUNDRY
D
W

MUD ROOM

KITCHEN
15'-0"x12'-0"

LIBRARY
15'-0"x24'-9"

GAMES ROOM
16'-0"x28'-0"

UP

BREAKFAST
15'-0"x13'-0"

GREAT ROOM
30'-0"x21'-0"

DN

DN

SCREENED PORCH
20'-10"x9'-0"

COVERED DECK

MAIN FLOOR

SECOND FLOOR

BEDROOM
11'-8"x11'-8"

BATH

BEDROOM
11'-8"x11'-8"

ENSUITE

W.I.C

W.I.C

LIN

LIN

DN

MASTER
BEDROOM
20'-0"x17'-6"

SITTING
ROOM
10'-0"x18'-0"

BALCONY
10'-0"x8'-0"

3,782 sq. ft

- This modern, three-bedroom cedar-sided home has a distinctive Victorian flavor with a large covered deck, turret and interesting roof lines. Note the original sunburst design above the upstairs window.

- The largely open main floor features a great room with a fireplace, octagonal seating area, library, breakfast room and spacious kitchen, with its island cooking range. A separate laundry room is found off the kitchen. The formal dining room also features a box-bay window. A large games room is also found on the main floor for the serious competitor.

- The second floor features an elegant master suite, with its own sitting room and balcony as well as two spacious closets and a five piece master bath. Two additional bedrooms share a full bathroom.

1,780 sq. ft.

- A combination of stone and cedar siding give this three-bedroom home a distinctive feeling. A gracious covered entry leads into a large foyer which opens into the open plan living and dining room, whose most striking feature is a large half-round window dominating one wall.

- In addition to a large well-appointed kitchen and a self-contained laundry room, the main floor also boasts a den or bedroom, with deck access and a full bath.

- The master bedroom, with its private deck and large closet, shares a bathroom with the second bedroom on the upper floor. A large corner tub, with windows on both sides, invites you to soak away the stresses of the day.

UPPER FLOOR

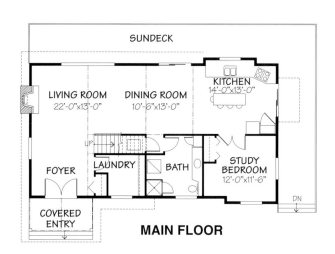

SUNDECK

LIVING ROOM
22'-0"x13'-0"

DINING ROOM
10'-6"x13'-0"

KITCHEN
14'-0"x13'-0"

UP

FOYER

LAUNDRY

BATH

STUDY
BEDROOM
12'-0"x11'-6"

DN

COVERED
ENTRY

MAIN FLOOR

MASTER
BEDROOM
18'-0"x13'-0"

BALCONY

DN

BEDROOM
12'-4"x11'-6"

SHARED
ENSUITE

Photography supplied by Design Bas

1,931 sq. ft.

- This compact, urban four bedroom charmer has a well-appointed master suite, with spa tub, double vanity and two walk-in closets.

- An imposing fireplace dominates the great room with its extra high ceiling.

- The gourmet kitchen opens into a spacious eating area with a bay window and a door to the garden.

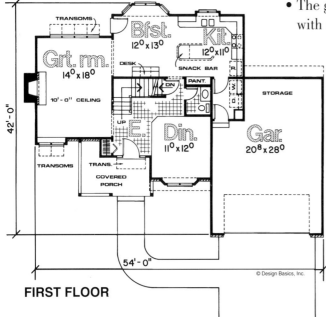

FIRST FLOOR

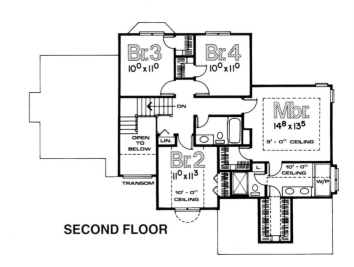

SECOND FLOOR

Photography by M+A Studio's

2,673 sq. ft.

- The welcoming veranda leads into the spacious entry foyer which divides the formal living and dining rooms.

- The large ground floor master suite occupies one side of this inviting five-bedroom home.   The ensuite includes spa tub and dual vanities, separate shower stall and ample closet space.

- There is an enormous family room, which features a corner fireplace, and opens on to the covered rear porch.

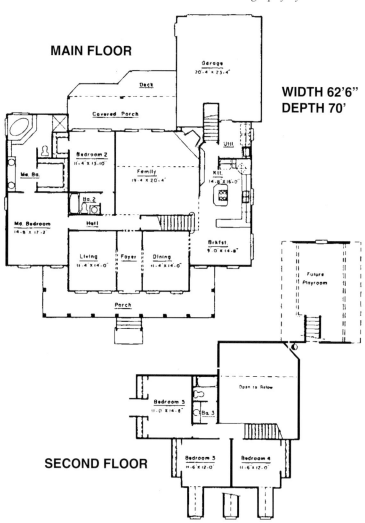

MAIN FLOOR

Garage
20·4 x 23·4

Deck

Covered Porch

WIDTH 62'6"
DEPTH 70'

Bedroom 2
11·4 x 13·10

Ma. Ba.

Family
19·4 x 20·4

Kit.
14·8 x 16·0

Ba. 2

Ma. Bedroom
14·8 x 17·2

Hall

Brkfst.
9·0 x 14·8

Living
11·4 x 14·0

Foyer

Dining
11·4 x 14·0

Porch

Future
Playroom

Open to Below

Bedroom 5
11·0 x 14·8

Ba. 3

SECOND FLOOR

Bedroom 3
11·6 x 12·0

Bedroom 4
11·6 x 12·0

2,458 sq. ft

- This truly exceptional three bedroom (or two bedroom and den) hor offers a wonderful range of features and amenities.

- The enormous master bedroom with adjoining ensuite and spacious his and hers walk-in closets, are neatly tucked away, offering the ultimate in privacy.

- The magnificent combination of vaulted living areas with prow fron design and wraparound balcony, brings year-round outdoor exposur

- Enjoy entertaining in your deluxe kitchen with island and adjacent living area.

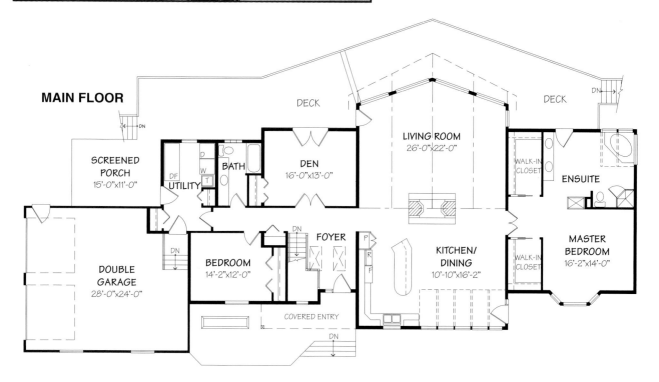

MAIN FLOOR

DECK

DECK

DN

LIVING ROOM
26'-0"x22'-0"

SCREENED
PORCH
15'-0"x11'-0"

DN

WALK-IN
CLOSET

DF
UTILITY

D
W

BATH

T

DEN
16'-0"x13'-0"

ENSUITE

DN

DN

BEDROOM
14'-2"x12'-0"

FOYER

P
R
F

KITCHEN/
DINING
10'-10"x16'-2"

WALK-IN
CLOSET

MASTER
BEDROOM
16'-2"x14'-0"

DOUBLE
GARAGE
28'-0"x24'-0"

COVERED ENTRY

DN

SECOND FLOOR

- BEDROOM 11'-10"x13'-8"
- MASTER BEDROOM 15'-0"x15'-8"
- ENSUITE
- WALK-IN CLOSET
- BATH
- DN
- BEDROOM 13'-0"x10'-4"
- BEDROOM 13'-6"x11'-2"
- OPEN TO BELOW

2,568 sq. ft

- This outstanding family home features all four bedrooms on the large upper level.

- The master bedroom boasts an ensuite with angled corner tub and generous walk-in closet.

- On the main floor there is the formal living room, cross-hall dining room, great room with fireplace, huge breakfast area, utility and mud rooms, and half-bathroom.

- BREAKFAST
- GEAT ROOM 29'-0"x15'-0"
- KITCHEN 12'-0"x14'-6"
- MUD ROOM
- UTILITY 9'-6"x10'-0"
- DN
- PAN
- LAV
- D W
- LIVING ROOM 13'-0"x19'-0"
- DINING ROOM 13'-6"x14'-4"
- DOUBLE GARAGE 24'-0"x24'-0"
- UP
- FOYER
- OPTIONAL SUNDECK

FIRST FLOOR

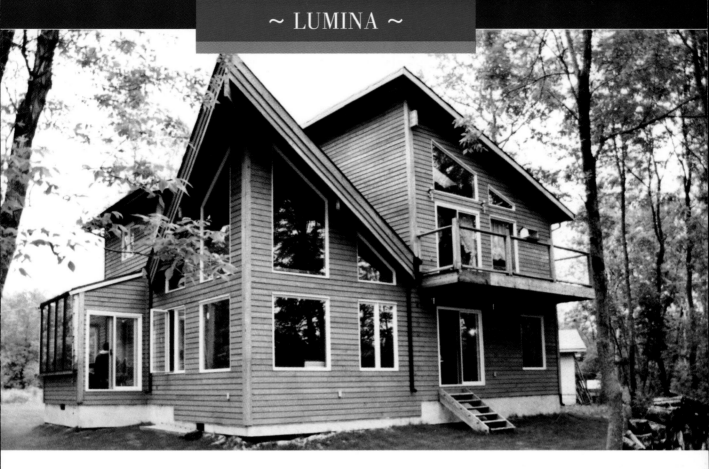

1,608 sq. ft.

- The exciting design of this impressive three-bedroom home features a unique angled prow, with an enormous expanse of windows, which provides a truly light and airy ambiance to the whole house.

- The conservatory-style dining room, with its glass panelled roof is directly adjacent to the well-appointed kitchen with its built-in breakfast bar.

- A feature staircase from the great room leads to the upper floor and to the master bedroom with its ensuite, walk-in closet, and a full-width balcony overlooking the deck below. Two additional bedrooms share a full bath on this floor.

SECOND FLOOR

BEDROOM
12'-0"x10'-0"

BATH

BATH

WALK-IN CLOSET

BEDROOM
10'-0"x12'-0"

DN

MASTER BEDROOM
16'-0"x12'-6"

OPEN TO BELOW

FOYER

D

W

BATH

KITCHEN
9'-0"x8'-0"

FAMILY ROOM
16'-0"x16'-0"

DN

DINING ROOM
13'-0"x12'-0"

UP

BALCONY

LIVING ROOM
16'-0"x12'-6"

FIRST FLOOR

Photography supplied by The Meredith Corporati

4,283 sq. ft

- The gracious open-plan main floor of this unique and appealing three-bedroom home offers generous great room, dining, kitchen and breakfast areas, all with deck access. A cozy den/library, laundry room, half-bath and breezeway complete the main floor.

- A central staircase leads to the second floor which includes a well-appointed master suite and two secondary bedrooms, each with private bath.

- A steeply pitched roof line and deep eaves, along with rounded windows, dormers and craftsman-style details contribute to the outstanding curb appeal of this home.

Photography supplied by The Meredith Corporation

Photography supplied by The Meredith Corporation

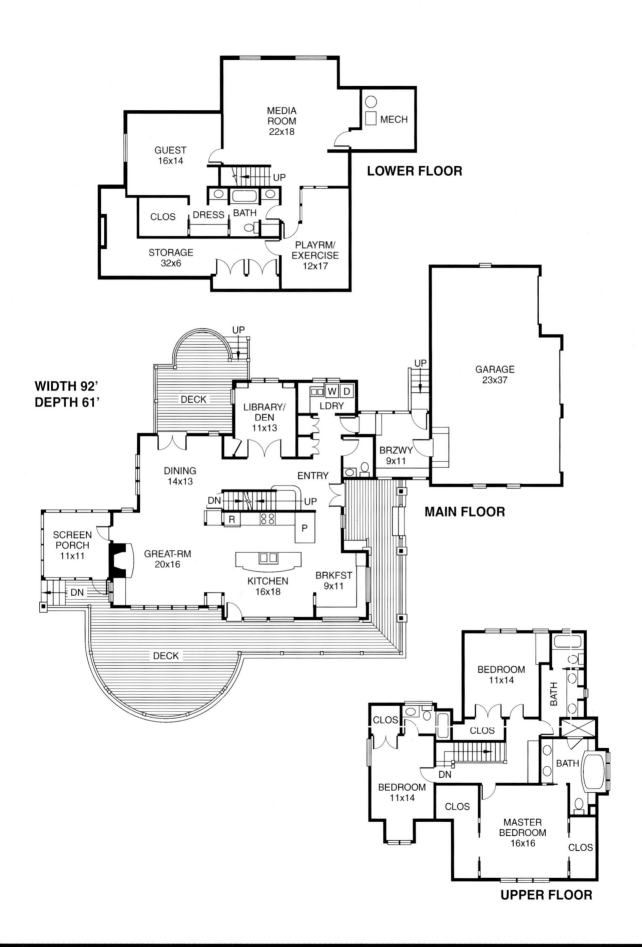

LOWER FLOOR

MEDIA ROOM 22x18

MECH

GUEST 16x14

UP

CLOS   DRESS   BATH

STORAGE 32x6

PLAYRM/ EXERCISE 12x17

WIDTH 92'
DEPTH 61'

UP

DECK

LIBRARY/ DEN 11x13

W D

LDRY

UP

GARAGE 23x37

BRZWY 9x11

DINING 14x13

ENTRY

MAIN FLOOR

DN   UP

R   P

SCREEN PORCH 11x11

GREAT-RM 20x16

KITCHEN 16x18

BRKFST 9x11

DN

DECK

BEDROOM 11x14

CLOS

BATH

CLOS

BEDROOM 11x14

DN

BATH

CLOS

MASTER BEDROOM 16x16

CLOS

UPPER FLOOR

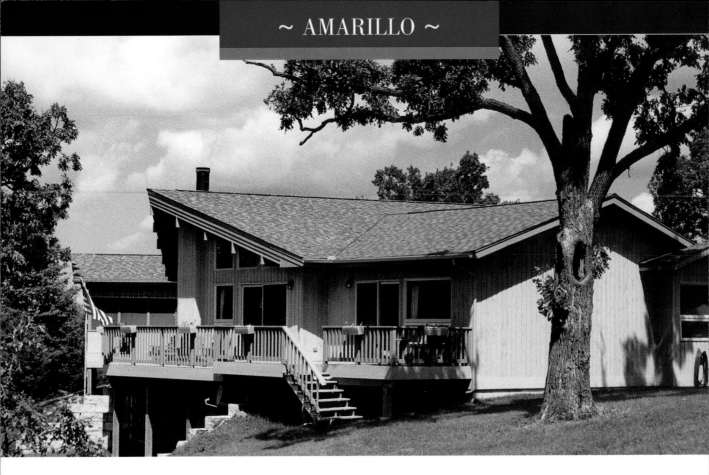

2,346 sq. ft

- This outstanding three-bedroom home features a totally private master bedroom wing with full ensuite, generous walk-in closet, and additional space.

- A feature fireplace stands between the vaulted living and dining areas with their magnificent prow windows.

- The large kitchen has ample cupboards, counter space and nook.

MAIN FLOOR

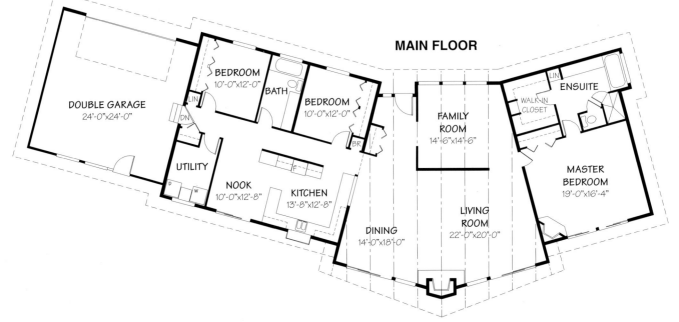

Photography by John Ehrenclou

2,541 sq. ft.

- This home combines the best of all worlds: a classic Victorian exterior and a four bedroom interior plan that more than answers the demands of modern family life.

- The angled kitchen, sunny breakfast bay, and hearth room flow together into a pleasing family space.

- Skylights and a vaulted ceiling bring a spectacular sky-lit atmosphere to the impressive living room which opens to the deck.

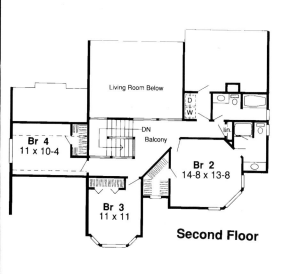

Second Floor

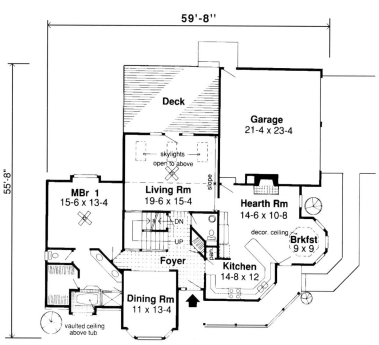

First Floor

Photography by John Ehrencl

2,083 sq. ft

- Picture a porch swing, cozy rocking chairs and a pitcher of lemonade on this country veranda. The formal areas of this traditional three bedroom home flank the entry hall.

- The well-appointed kitchen is divided from the family room by a breakfast bar. A mud room with garden and garage access, laundry room and guest bathroom complete the main floor.

- In addition to the three bedrooms the upper floor features a window seat framed by built-in bookshelves, providing a cozy place to curl up with a book.

SECOND FLOOR

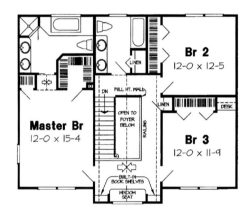

Br 2
12-0 x 12-5

Master Br
12-0 x 15-4

Br 3
12-0 x 11-9

LINEN

FULL HT. WALL

DN

OPEN TO FOYER BELOW

RAILING

LINEN

DESK

BUILT-IN BOOK SHELVES

WINDOW SEAT

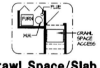

Crawl Space/Slab Option

FLUE

FURN

W.H.

CRAWL SPACE ACCESS

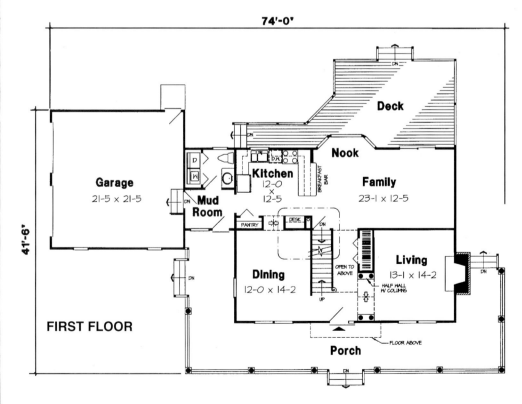

74'-0"

41'-6"

FIRST FLOOR

Garage
21-5 x 21-5

Mud Room

Kitchen
12-0 x 12-5

Breakfast Bar

Nook

Deck

Family
23-1 x 12-5

Pantry

DESK

Dining
12-0 x 14-2

OPEN TO ABOVE

UP

DN

Living
13-1 x 14-2

HALF WALL W/ COLUMNS

FLOOR ABOVE

Porch

D W

DN

1,320 sq. ft

- The splendid windows in the vaulted living areas seem to bring the outdoors into this elegant two-storey chalet.

- In addition to the open-plan living and dining room, the main floor features one private bedroom, a three-piece bath, laundry room, and a very functional kitchen with nook by the window.

- Two more bedrooms, a cozy loft open to the living areas, and a full bath are situated on the second level.

BEDROOM
12'-0"x12'-0"

BEDROOM
9'-8"x12'-0"

DN

BATH

OPEN TO MAIN FLOOR

UPPER FLOOR

BEDROOM
14'-0"x10'-4"

BATH

UTILITY

W D

UP

F R

KITCHEN
16'-0"x12'-0"

LIVING ROOM
14'-0"x20'-0"

DINING ROOM
16'-0"x12'-0"

MAIN FLOOR

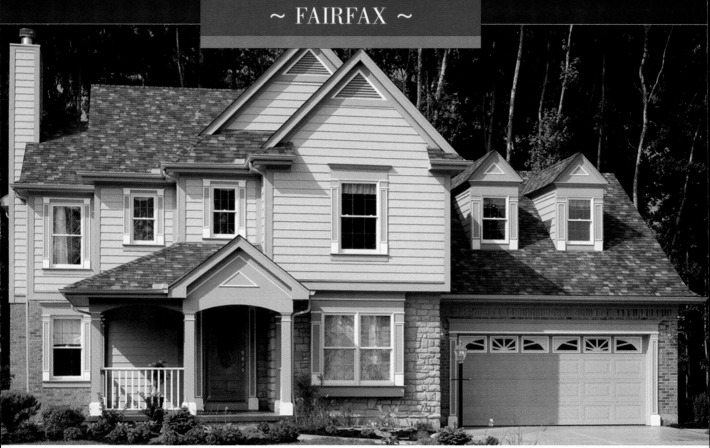

Photography by Donna & Ron Kolb Exposures Unlimited

1,898 sq. ft.

- The sunken great room of this three bedroom home features a wood burning fireplace and a built-in entertainment centre.

- Ample windows in the great room and adjoining breakfast room provide a light and airy atmosphere.

- The second floor offers a generous master bedroom ensuite and two secondary bedrooms, another bathroom and a large bonus room over the garage.

SECOND FLOOR

FIRST FLOOR

1,579 sq. ft.

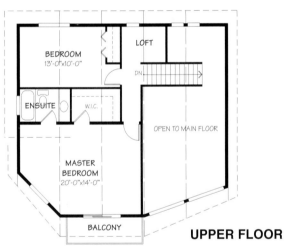

BEDROOM
13'-0"x10'-0"

LOFT

ENSUITE

W.I.C.

DN

OPEN TO MAIN FLOOR

MASTER
BEDROOM
20'-0"x14'-0"

BALCONY

UPPER FLOOR

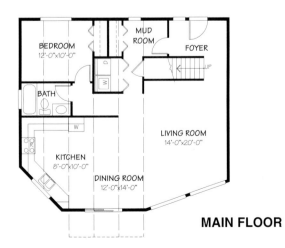

BEDROOM
12'-0"x10'-0"

MUD
ROOM

FOYER

BATH

UP

LIVING ROOM
14'-0"x20'-0"

KITCHEN
8'-0"x10'-0"

W

DINING ROOM
12'-0"x14'-0"

MAIN FLOOR

- An impressive foyer leads into this spectacular three bedroom home, with a front-oriented upper master bedroom highlighted by a dazzling cathedral window, private ensuite, and walk-in closet.

- The second level is completed by a second bedroom and cozy loft.

- The main floor features a delightful open-plan living room, dining area and fantastic kitchen; a third bedroom, full bath, mudroom and a utility area complete the plan.

Photography by John Ehrenclou

3,276 sq. ft.

- Well-placed skylights and abundant windows bathe every room in sunlight in this spectacular four bedroom family home.

- The wide open family area at the rear of the house includes the kitchen, breakfast room and family room with fireplace, built-in bar and bookshelves.

- The two-story foyer features an open staircase leading to the bedrooms on the upper floor.

SECOND FLOOR

FIRST FLOOR

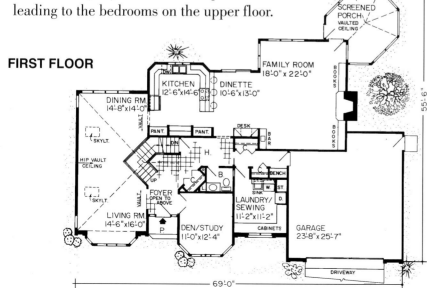

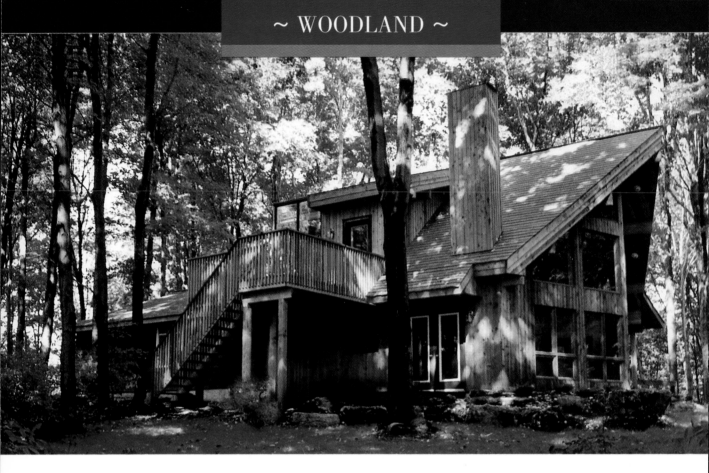

1,489 sq. ft

- This beautiful open-plan home boasts vaulted living areas with prow windows, a large feature fireplace and two very private bedrooms.

- The second level master bedroom, with full ensuite and enormous walk-in closet, enjoys access to a commanding sundeck.

- Other amenities on the main level include laundry room, full bath, the second bedroom and a kitchen designed for the serious chef.

UPPER FLOOR   **MAIN FLOOR**

2,875 sq. ft.

- Large windows, impressive decks and porches, a stunning great room, a beautiful loft and large beam accents make this design the epitome of log home style. A large kitchen, fit for the most discriminating of chefs, is tucked conveniently away from the more formal living areas of the great room.

- The master suite and secondary bedroom, each complete with en suite, are isolated in separate wings for total seclusion. A spacious third room can be used for home office, den or family room. This design is extremely flexible-easily adapted to any family's needs.

UPPER FLOOR   **MAIN FLOOR**

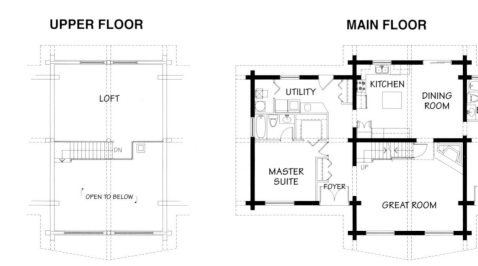

1,187 sq. ft

- This unique getaway retreat features two very private bedrooms.

- Many picture windows and skylights facilitate the flow of natural light from all directions.

- The stunning spiral staircase adds architectural interest to this truly one-of-a-kind home design.

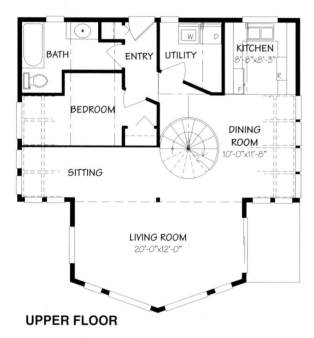

BATH

ENTRY   UTILITY

KITCHEN
8'-8"x8'-3"

W   D

BEDROOM

DINING
ROOM
10'-0"x11'-8"

SITTING

LIVING ROOM
20'-0"x12'-0"

UPPER FLOOR

BALCONY

BEDROOM / LOFT

OPEN TO BELOW

MAIN FLOOR

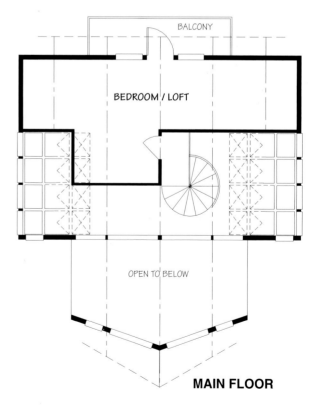

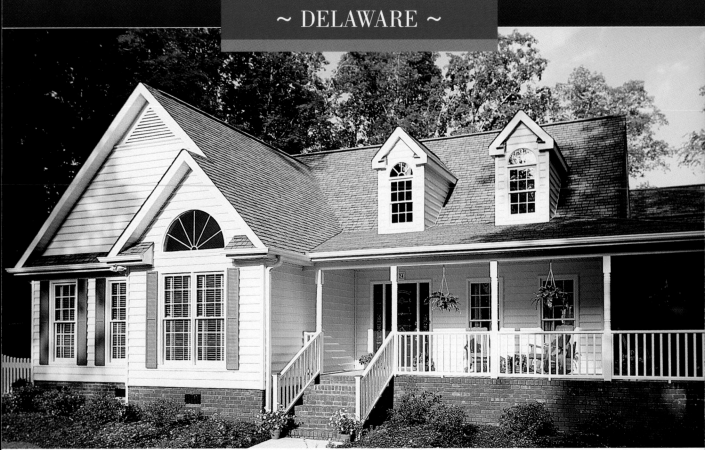

Photography by Jon Riley, Riley & Riley Photograph

1,815 sq. ft.

- This attractive three bedroom country cottage, with gables, offers ample one-floor living space.

- The large master bedroom has its own ensuite and walk-in closet. The great room and kitchen share a vaulted cathedral ceiling.

- The wrap-around front porch, breakfast bay window and skylit back porch add charm and expand the living space.

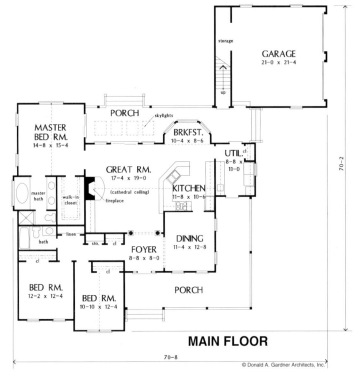

MAIN FLOOR

© Donald A. Gardner Architects, Inc.

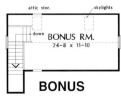

BONUS

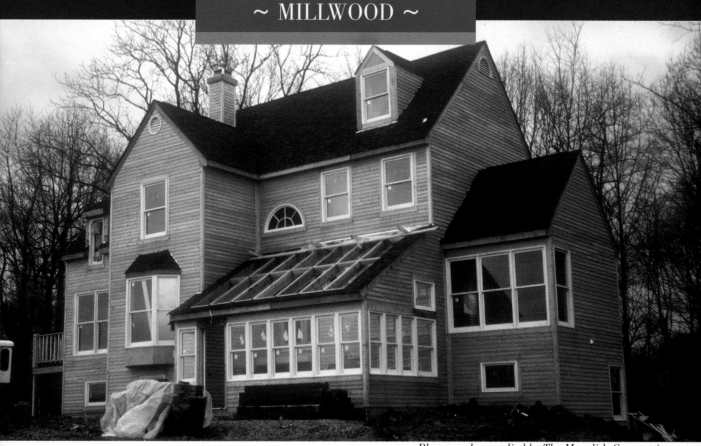

Photography supplied by The Meredith Corporation

2,558 sq. ft.

- A two-story solarium and a morning room are features of this character four bedroom home.

- The second floor master bedroom has an adjoining private sitting room, with a spiral staircase to the main floor den.

- Many windows, including bay, half-round and dormers capture light and warmth from the sun.

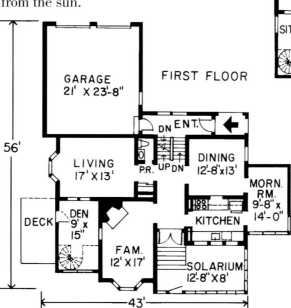

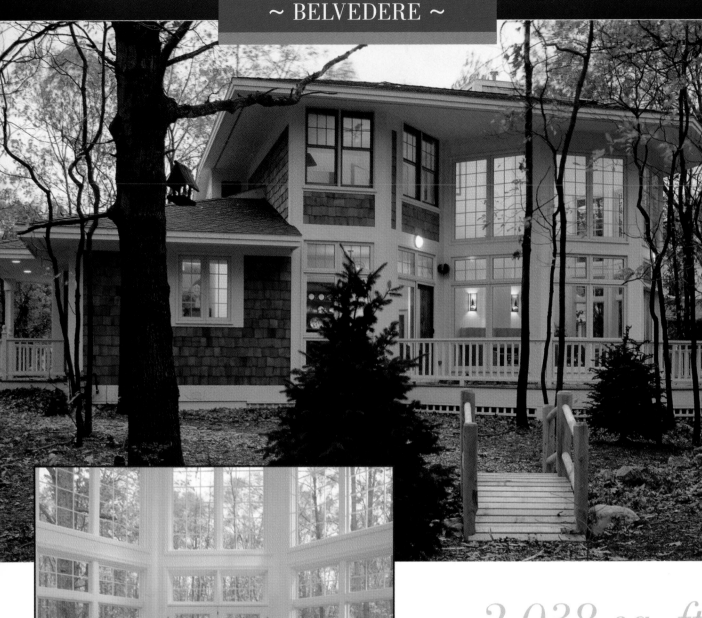

Photography supplied by The Meredith Corporation

2,038 sq. ft

- An eight foot wide deck wraps around much of this home and, combined with a screened porch, enhances the outdoor living space of this gorgeous three bedroom house.

- The master bedroom is located on the main floor with two additional bedrooms upstairs.

- The octagonal shaped living room has a soaring expanse of glass and the enormous windows let the sunlight flood in to highlight the beautiful interior finishing.

Photography supplied by The Meredith Corporation

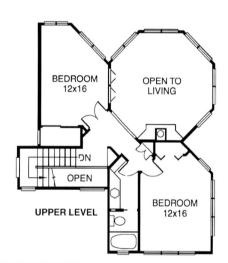

BEDROOM
12x16

OPEN TO LIVING

DN

OPEN

BEDROOM
12x16

UPPER LEVEL

WIDTH 46'4"
DEPTH 37'8"

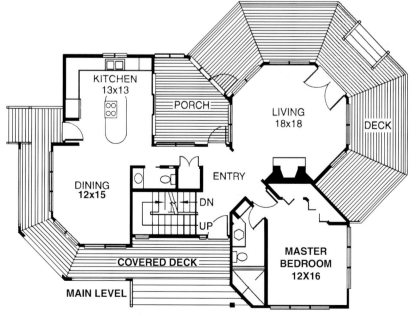

KITCHEN
13x13

PORCH

LIVING
18x18

DECK

DINING
12x15

ENTRY

DN

UP

MASTER
BEDROOM
12X16

COVERED DECK

MAIN LEVEL

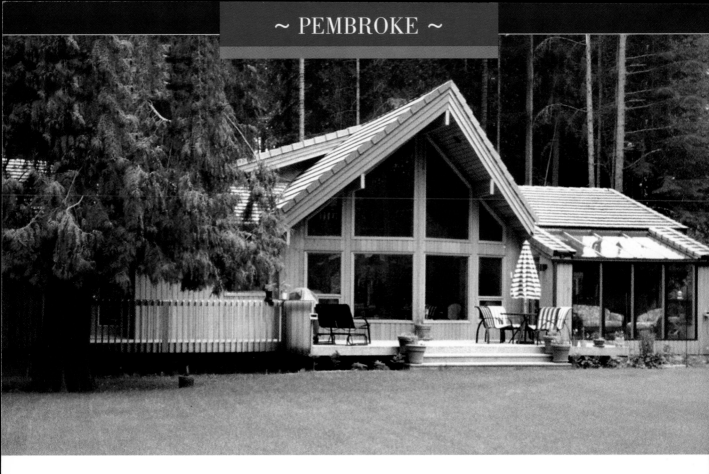

2,109 sq. ft.

- This contemporary classic offers a hideaway bedroom or den on the second floor.

- The master bedroom with full ensuite and walk-in closet and a third bedroom are conveniently situated on the main level.

- The great room living area features a massive expanded-prow window design and the dining room has french doors opening on to the optional deck.

UPPER FLOOR

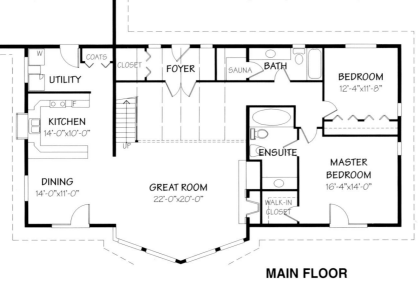

DOUBLE GARAGE
24'-0"x24'-0"

W

COATS
CLOSET

UTILITY

FOYER

SAUNA

BATH

BEDROOM
12'-4"x11'-8"

UPPER FLOOR

DN

CLOSET

BEDROOM OR DEN
18'-0"x15'-0"

KITCHEN
14'-0"x10'-0"

UP

ENSUITE

MASTER BEDROOM
16'-4"x14'-0"

OPEN TO GREAT ROOM

DINING
14'-0"x11'-0"

GREAT ROOM
22'-0"x20'-0"

WALK-IN CLOSET

MAIN FLOOR

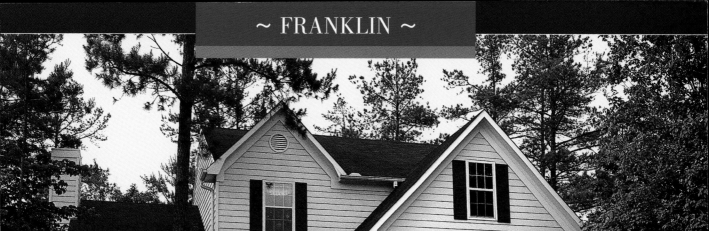

Photography by John Ehrenclou

1,944 sq. ft.

- This cozy and appealing three bedroom family home offers many amenities found in bigger homes.

- The vaulted ceiling and large windows provide a spacious airy atmosphere in the master bedroom, which features an attached bathroom with whirlpool and walk-in closet.

- In addition to two other bedrooms, the upper floor provides a bonus room over the garage.

Slab/Crawl Space Plan

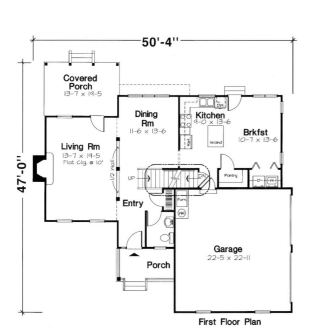

First Floor Plan

Second Floor Plan

4,326 sq. ft

- This large and distinctive five bedroom home features an expansive vaulted dining and living area with fireplace and enormous windows— perfect for entertaining.

- Located in its own private wing, the huge master bedroom offers a corner fireplace, full ensuite with windowed-alcove tub, very generous walk-in closet, and secluded balcony.

- Other highlights include a superb island kitchen adjacent to the family room (with a third fireplace), covered porch, mudroom, two bedrooms with ensuite half-baths on the main level, and two more bedrooms up, with a full bath and roomy loft.

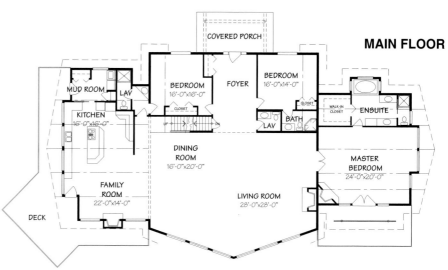

MAIN FLOOR

COVERED PORCH

MUD ROOM

LAV

BEDROOM
16'-0"x16'-0"

FOYER

BEDROOM
16'-0"x14'-0"

CLOSET

WALK-IN
CLOSET

ENSUITE

KITCHEN
16'-0"x16'-0"

CLOSET

LAV

BATH

FAMILY
ROOM
22'-0"x14'-0"

DINING
ROOM
16'-0"x20'-0"

MASTER
BEDROOM
24'-0"x20'-0"

DECK

LIVING ROOM
28'-0"x28'-0"

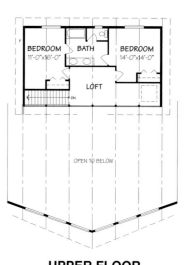

BEDROOM
11'-0"x16'-0"

BATH

BEDROOM
14'-0"x14'-0"

LOFT

DN

OPEN TO BELOW

UPPER FLOOR

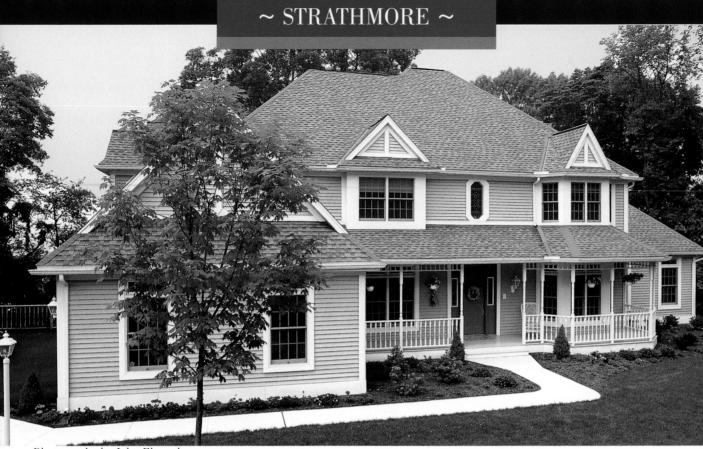

Photography by John Ehrenclou

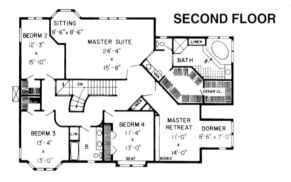

SECOND FLOOR

SITTING
8'-6" x 8'-6"

BEDRM. 2
12'-3"
x
15'-10"

MASTER SUITE
24'-4"
x
15'-8"

LINEN

BATH

BEDRM. 3
13'-4"
x
13'-0"

LIN

B.

BEDRM.4
11'-4"
x
13'-0"
SEAT

MASTER
RETREAT
11'-0"
x
14'-0"
BOOKS

DORMER
8'-6" x 7'-0"

CEDAR CL.

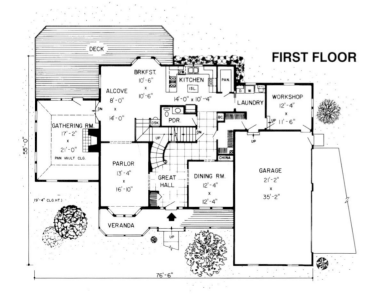

FIRST FLOOR

DECK

BRKFST.
10'-6"
x
10'-6"

KITCHEN
14'-0" x 10'-4"
ISL

PAN.

ALCOVE
8'-0"
x
14'-0"

LAUNDRY

WORKSHOP
12'-4"
x
11'-6"

GATHERING RM.
17'-2"
x
21'-0"
PAN VAULT CLG.

PDR.

DSK

BC

PARLOR
13'-4"
x
16'-0"

GREAT
HALL

DINING RM.
12'-4"
x
12'-4"

CHINA

GARAGE
21'-2"
x
35'-2"

VERANDA

(9'-4" CLG. HT.)

55'-0"

76'-6"

4,217 sq. ft.

- The main floor of this elegant, Victorian style, four bedroom home provides ample space for entertaining. In addition to a formal parlour and dining room divided by an impressive entry foyer, the main floor offers an enormous sunken gathering room, with vaulted ceiling and windows on all sides.

- Other main floor features include a large kitchen with a sunny breakfast room, a separate pantry, laundry room and workshop. A large walk-in closet off the laundry room provides invaluable extra storage space.

- On the upper floor is the master suite with its separate sitting area and generous walk-in cedar closets. A unique feature of the master suite is a book-lined retreat with dormered sitting area. Three additional bedrooms on this floor share a full bathroom.

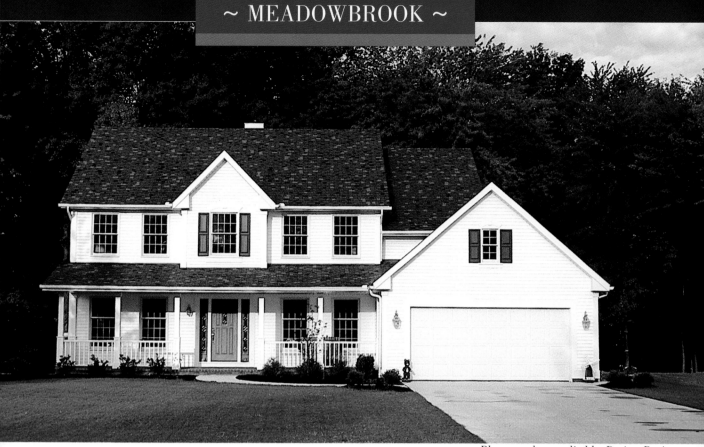

Photography supplied by Design Basics

2,644 sq. ft.

- The large bay-windowed family room, with built-in entertainment centre, shares a see-through fireplace with the breakfast room of this family-oriented, four bedroom home.

- The gourmet kitchen features a cook top island and pantry and is adjacent to a separate laundry room. In the dining room, a built-in hutch provides additional storage space.

- Upstairs, there are three good-sized bedrooms that share a large double-vanitied bathroom. The master suite offers high ceilings and a large ensuite with a whirlpool tub and a skylight for maximum light.

SECOND FLOOR

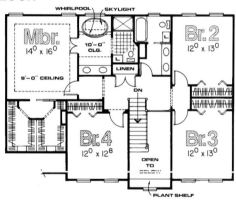

FIRST FLOOR

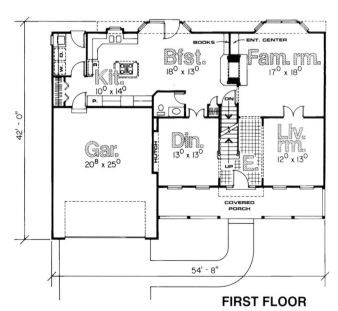

Photography supplied by The Meredith Corporation

4,823 sq. ft

- A beautiful front porch provides a warm welcome to this four bedroom Victorian farmhouse. Two turrets create sunlit rooms on both the front and back of the house. The spacious living room shares a fireplace with an expansive family room.

- A multi-windowed breakfast room adjoins the well-appointed kitchen which opens on to the covered side porch. The unique, gazebo-style dining room also overlooks the side porch. A separate laundry room and small powder room complete the main floor.

- The large second floor master bedroom features five signature windows, well-appointed ensuite and a generous walk-in closet. Three additional bedrooms on this floor share two full bathrooms.

- A large, well-equipped media room, occupying one wing of the upper floor, is reached by a second staircase from the main floor.

Photography supplied by The Meredith Corporation

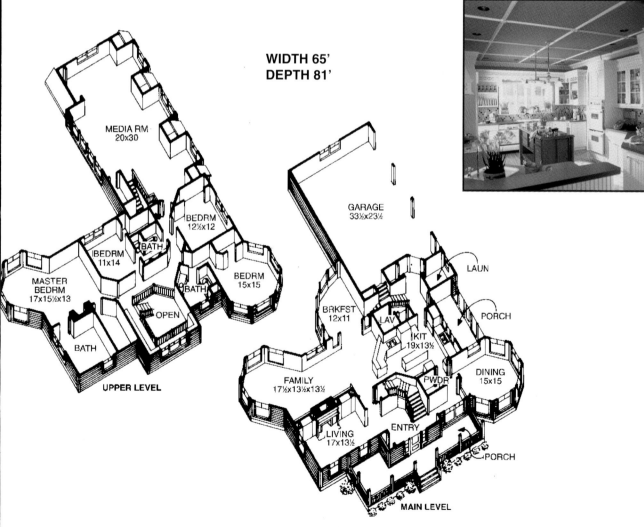

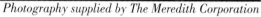

WIDTH 65'
DEPTH 81'

MEDIA RM
20x30

GARAGE
33½x23½

BEDRM
12½x12

BATH

BEDRM
11x14

BEDRM
15x15

LAUN

MASTER
BEDRM
17x15½x13

BATH

OPEN

BRKFST
12x11

LAV

PORCH

KIT
19x13½

BATH

DINING
15x15

UPPER LEVEL

FAMILY
17½x13½x13½

PWDR

LIVING
17x13½

ENTRY

PORCH

MAIN LEVEL

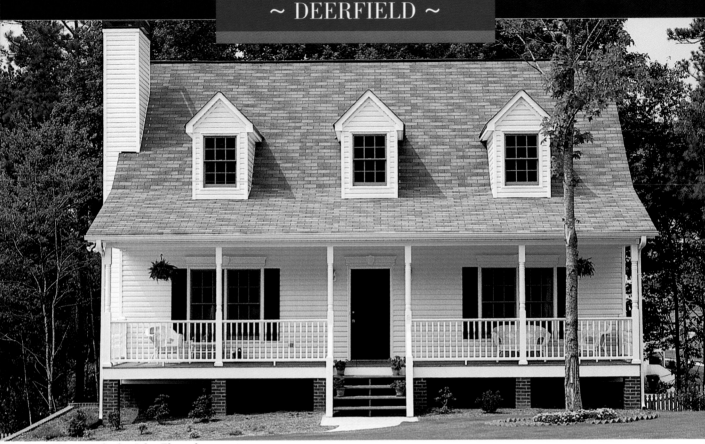

Photography by John Ehrenclou

SECOND FLOOR

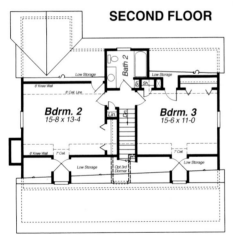

1,668 sq. ft.

- This cozy three bedroom home has immediate appeal with its charming old-fashioned country porch.

- A first floor master suite, including a luxurious master bath, ensures privacy as the two additional bedrooms are located on the second floor. These second floor bedrooms are both large and have ample closet space. Additional roof storage is accessible on each side of both bedrooms.

- The well-designed floor space efficiently combines an open plan living and dining area, accented by a welcoming fireplace. The kitchen and breakfast room open to a rear sundeck, expanding into outdoor living space.

FIRST FLOOR

1,932 sq. ft.

- This sophisticated design illustrates an efficient use of floor space that includes two large bedrooms.

- The private upper floor master bedroom is complete with a full ensuite, spacious walk-in closet and balcony.

- The high cathedral ceilings and prow-style glass front adds to the open, airy feeling of this home.

FIRST FLOOR

DOUBLE GARAGE
24'-0"x23'-0"

UTILITY

BEDROOM
16'-0"x11'-6"

BATH

PAN F   R
KITCHEN
14'-0"x13'-8"

UP

SECOND FLOOR

WALK-IN
CLOSET
DRESSING

MASTER
BEDROOM
16'-2"x19'-6"

ENSUITE

DN

LOFT
14'-0"x12'-0"

OPEN TO BELOW

LIVING ROOM
14'-0"x19'-0"

DINING ROOM
14'-0"x12'-0"

SUNDECK

1,834 sq. ft

- The warmth of timber and the coziness of a stone fireplace enhance the appeal of this unique three-bedroom log home. A large covered porch along the front of the house provides plenty of shade for those warm days, while giving the feel of outdoor living. Throughout the house the open interior beams promote a feeling of space and rustic charm.

- The entry foyer emphasizes the open floor plan design, featuring a large living room with its impressive stone fireplace. The dining room is open to the living room and to the large country-style kitchen with its peninsula, plentiful counter space and pantry. Sliding doors from the dining area lead to a small covered porch, allowing a breeze to circulate during hot weather. A comfortable den and a bedroom with adjoining full bath complete the main floor.

- The upper floor, which is partly open to the downstairs foyer, is dominated by two large bedrooms, both overlooking the front porch. These rooms share a full bath and each has ample closet space.

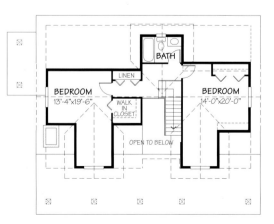

MAIN FLOOR

COVERED PORCH
6'-0"x9'-4"

DINING ROOM
11'-8"x14'-4"

KITCHEN
13'-8"x14'-4"

BEDROOM
14'-0"x12'-0"

BATH

LIVING ROOM
19'-8"x13'-8"

FOYER

UP

DEN/UTILITY
10'-8"x10'-6"

COVERED PORCH
42'-6"x7'-0"

UPPER FLOOR

BATH

LINEN

BEDROOM
13'-4"x19'-6"

WALK IN CLOSET

BEDROOM
14'-0"x20'-0"

OPEN TO BELOW

Photography supplied by Design Basics

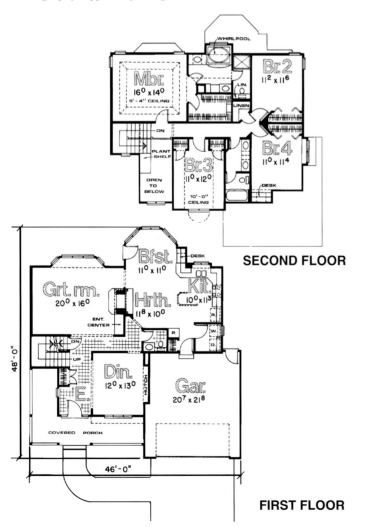

SECOND FLOOR

FIRST FLOOR

2,270 sq. ft

- The main floor of this four bedroom family home features a great room which lives up to its name. A built-in entertainment centre, a see-through fireplace, shared with the hearth room, and an elegant bay window highlight this room.

- The open layout of the hearth room, breakfast room with its gazebo-style windows and built-in desk, and the kitchen, with its pantry and separate laundry room, give an airy feeling to this living space.

- The upper floor of the dramatic two-storey entry opens into the luxurious master suite, with its lavish ensuite, whirlpool and generous walk-in closet. Three additional bedrooms share a double-vanitied full bathroom on this floor.

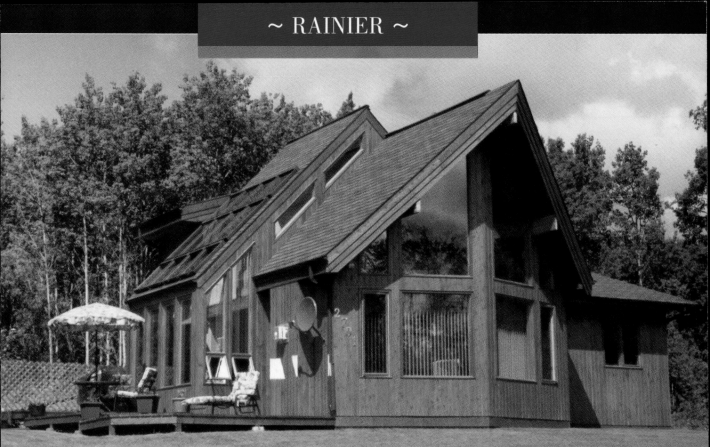

1,442 sq. ft.

- This interesting three bedroom design is a long-time favorite.

- Natural light streams through glorious two-story solarium windows into the secluded upper-level master bedroom.

- Exceptional features include the vaulted living room with gigantic prow windows, dining room/solarium area, and the absolute dream kitchen.

FIRST FLOOR

KITCHEN
12'-0"x10'-0"

ENTRY

R   F

PANTRY

UTILITY

D
W

BEDROOM
9'-8"x9'-8"

SOLARIUM / DINING
18'-0"x12'-0"

UP

BATH

BEDROOM
9'-8"x9'-8"

LIVING ROOM
20'-0"x11'-0"

SECOND FLOOR

MASTER
BEDROOM
13'-6"x20'-0"

ENSUITE

WALK-IN
CLOSET

DN

OPEN TO LIVING ROOM

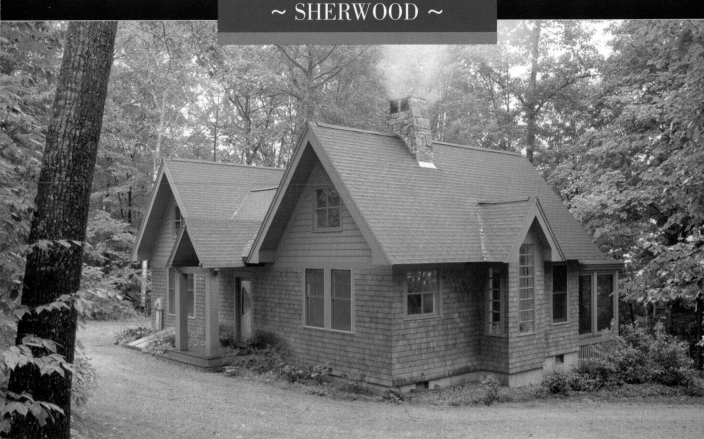

Photography supplied by The Meredith Corporation

1,112 sq. ft

- High ceilings and gable windows give the interior of this cozy woodland cottage a light and airy feeling.

- A gracious entry hall separates the two bedrooms from the living room and kitchen.

- The courtyard deck, a screened porch off the living room and a large rear deck expand the living space outdoors.

- The spacious living room features a fireplace, built-in entertainment centre and a beautiful box-bay window.

MAIN FLOOR

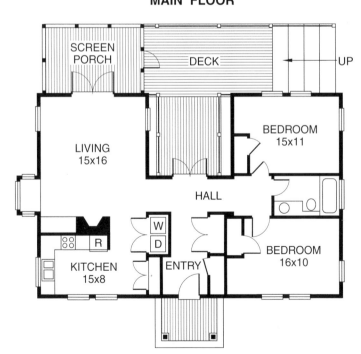

WIDTH 47'
DEPTH 45'6"

Photography supplied by The Meredith Corporation

1,881 sq. ft.

- An inviting veranda and varied rooflines add to the appeal of this two bedroom with den, or three bedroom New England cottage.

- The open plan kitchen, dining and living room flow together to create an open and airy atmosphere.

- The bay window in the kitchen fills the working space with ample natural light.

- The upper floor offers a large master bedroom and a good sized second bedroom, each with a full private bathroom.

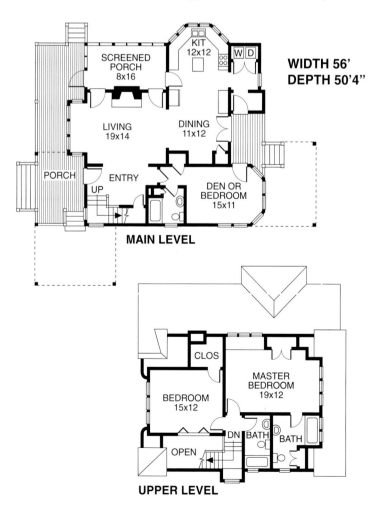

WIDTH 56'
DEPTH 50'4"

SCREENED PORCH 8x16

KIT 12x12

W D

LIVING 19x14

DINING 11x12

PORCH

ENTRY

UP

DEN OR BEDROOM 15x11

MAIN LEVEL

CLOS

MASTER BEDROOM 19x12

BEDROOM 15x12

DN BATH BATH

OPEN

UPPER LEVEL

1,523 sq. ft

- Imagine yourself in this enchanting log hideaway! Perfect as a full time residence or a weekend getaway, this single floor home is compact, complete and practical, with many features normally found in a much larger home.

- A spacious foyer features ample storage area, and a large utility room is adjacent to the secluded kitchen. Three large, private bedrooms and plenty of windows give this home the grace, charm and practicality that make it a memorable design.

MAIN FLOOR

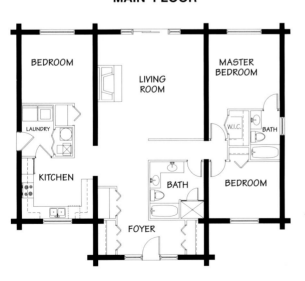

BEDROOM

LIVING ROOM

MASTER BEDROOM

LAUNDRY

W.I.C.

BATH

KITCHEN

BATH

BEDROOM

FOYER

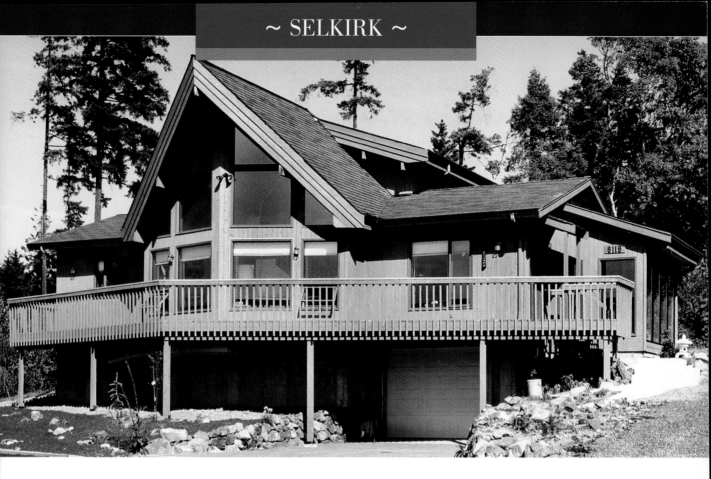

1,637 sq. ft.

- This spacious, three-bedroom home demonstrates elegance and charm, accentuated by a large open plan dining and kitchen area.

- The dazzling combination of vaulted living areas, extensive use of glass, and wraparound balcony provides an outdoor feeling throughout the home.

- The upper master bedroom offers absolute privacy, with the luxury of an ensuite and walk-in closet.

- A superb sunroom has been added to bring the natural beauty of the outdoors closer.

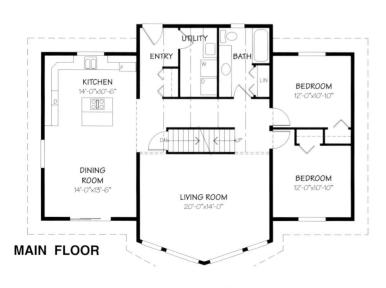

MAIN FLOOR

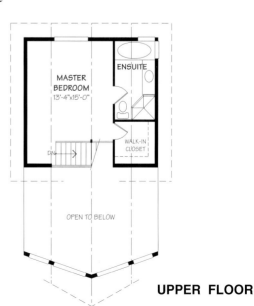

UPPER FLOOR

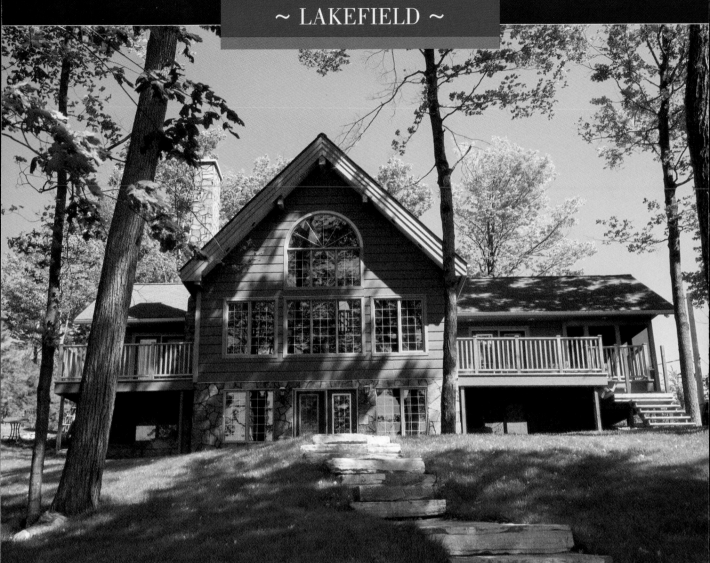

PHOTO: A. PARKIN

1,873 sq. ft

- This beautiful post and beam home is meticulously crafted and finished on the exterior with top quality log siding. The great room, with a huge gabled wall of glass, has massive fir beams, together with pine liner which gives it an imposing yet warm and intimate feeling. The large gourmet kitchen shares views of both the front and back of the property. Perfect for formal or casual living.

- This design expands the whole concept of cedar homes.

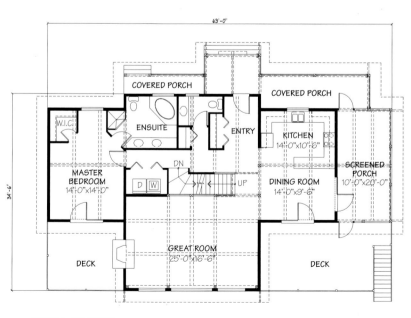

MAIN FLOOR

- COVERED PORCH
- COVERED PORCH
- W.I.C.
- ENSUITE
- ENTRY
- KITCHEN 14'-0"x10'-6"
- SCREENED PORCH 10'-0"x20'-0"
- MASTER BEDROOM 14'-0"x14'-0"
- DN
- UP
- D
- W
- DINING ROOM 14'-0"x9'-6"
- DECK
- GREAT ROOM 25'-0"x16'-6"
- DECK
- 63'-0"
- 34'-6"

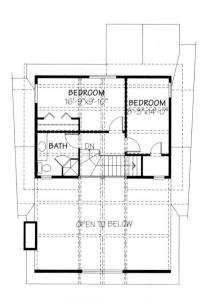

UPPER FLOOR

- BEDROOM 16'-9"x9'-10"
- BEDROOM 16'-3"x14'-0"
- BATH
- DN
- OPEN TO BELOW

1,440 sq. ft

- This three-bedroom chalet finds all three bedrooms conveniently located on the upper floor.

- The master bedroom boasts his and hers closets and a private front-facing balcony.

- The layout of the living areas with sundeck permits individual family members to enjoy their own privacy.

UPPER FLOOR

MAIN FLOOR

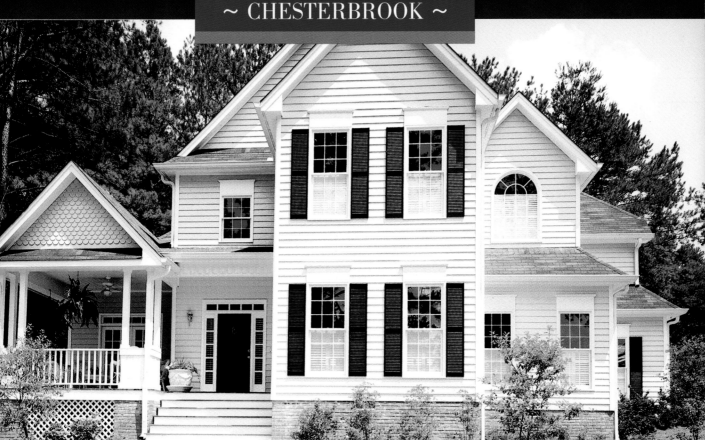

Photography by Joel Whisenant

3,013 sq. ft.

- Decorative shutters and large windows accentuate the appeal of this impressive four-bedroom home. Wide steps lead to the entrance hall which opens into the open plan living and dining areas and into the family room.

- The large family room is highlighted by a cozy fireplace and offers access to the sunny breakfast room. Doors from the family room lead to both the front porch and the rear deck. A roomy, well-appointed kitchen and half bath round out the main floor.

- The spacious second floor features two master suites, each with an ensuite and large walk-in closet. Two additional bedrooms share a full bath. In addition, the upper floor boasts a large laundry room with generous storage space.

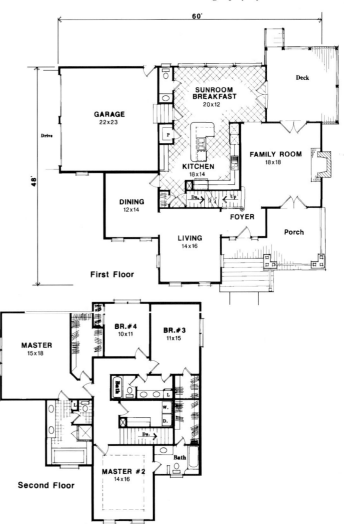

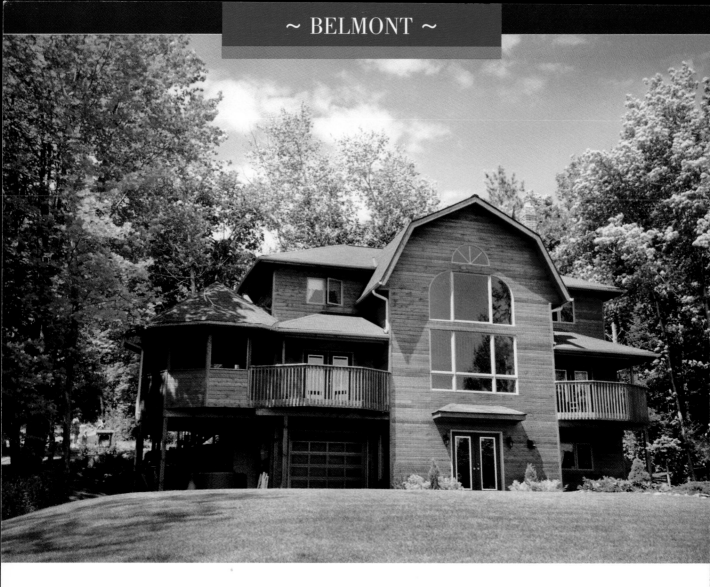

2,190 sq. ft

- A very distinctive roof line and windows, two covered porches, and a charming gazebo distinguish this spectacular four-bedroom residence.

- The master bedroom, featuring a spacious walk-in closet and full ensuite with corner shower, plus two additional private bedrooms and bath, are situated on the second floor.

- Main floor amenities include an impressive entry, laundry-storage room, a large bedroom with walk-in closet adjacent to a full bath. The superb U-shaped kitchen, living and dining areas are designed for family or entertaining.

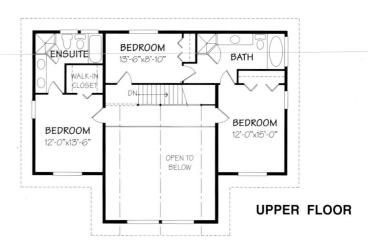

UPPER FLOOR

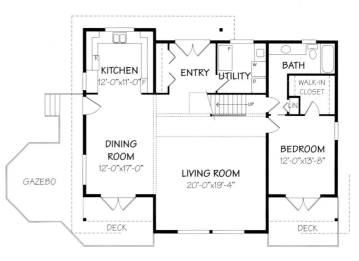

MAIN FLOOR

Photography supplied by Design Basics

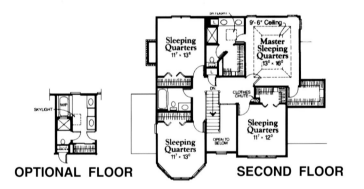

OPTIONAL FLOOR   **SECOND FLOOR**

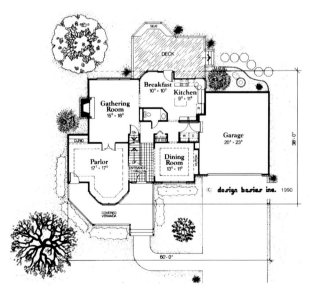

FIRST FLOOR

2,392 sq. ft.

- An enticing veranda and inviting portico lead into this gracious and well-designed four-bedroom home. The formal parlour and one of the upstairs bedrooms have the added charm of gazebo windows.

- Elegant french doors lead from the parlour to the large family/gathering room with its cozy fireplace and bright window wall. The kitchen, with its work island and wraparound counters, incorporates a comfortable breakfast area leading to the large rear deck.

- A generous, high-ceilinged master bedroom with its skylit master ensuite and two walk-in closets, shares the upper floor with three additional bedrooms and a full bath.

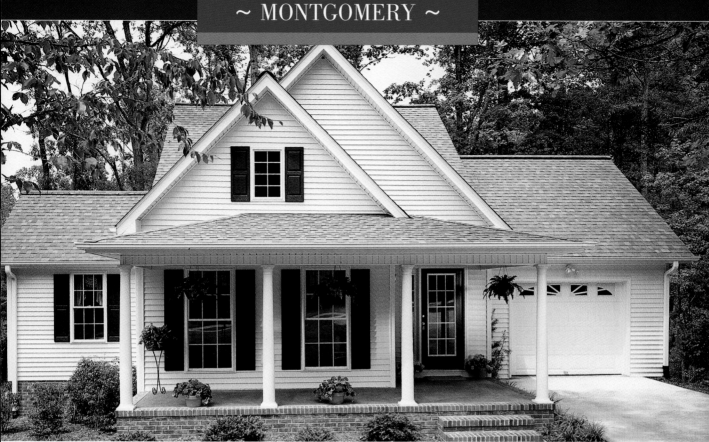

Photography by Jon Riley, Riley & Riley Photography

1,558 sq. ft.

- This appealing, three-bedroom traditional home is surprisingly spacious. Its two-storey foyer offers a welcome to the great room with its cathedral ceiling and fireplace.

- The efficiently-designed floor plan allows an easy flow between the great room, dining room and kitchen, with its adjacent utility/laundry room and access to the rear deck.

- The master suite is secluded at the rear of the house and includes a generous walk-in closet and private ensuite with separate shower and corner tub.

- On the upper floor two additional bedrooms share a full bathroom. This floor also provides attic storage space.

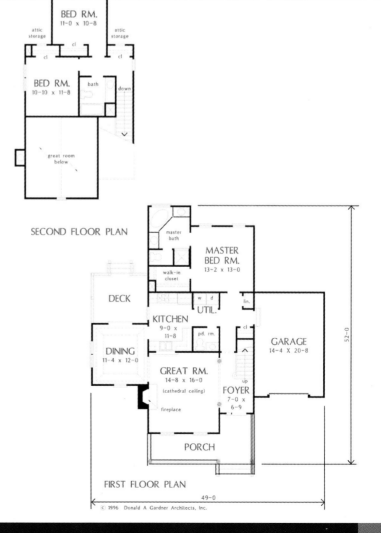

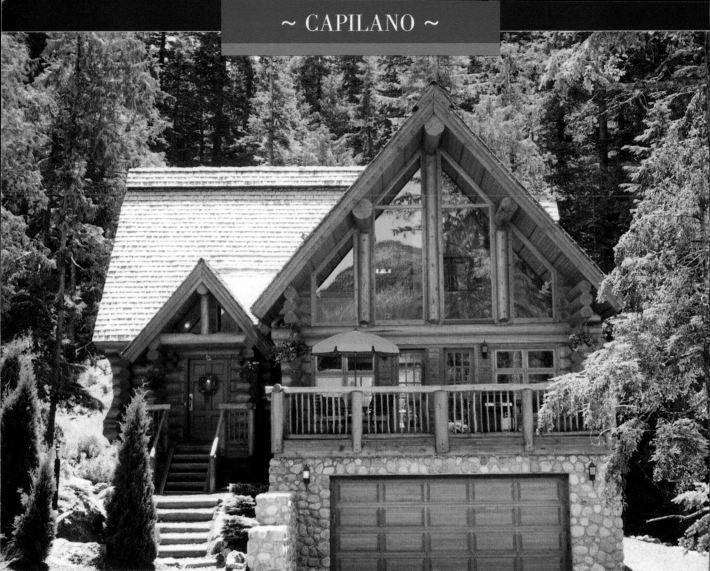

PHOTO: A. PARKIN

1,584 sq. ft

- Sunlight streams through the impressive windows of the living room in this attractive family home.

- An open plan main floor is ideal for entertaining. The bedroom on this level can be used as a study or home office.

- The master bedroom with its own dressing room and bathroom is upstairs and is spaciously separated from the other guest bedroom.

- A family home designed for gracious living.

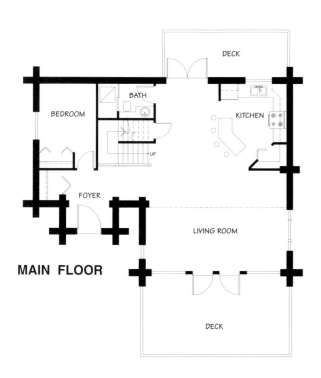

UPPER FLOOR

DECK

BATH

BEDROOM

KITCHEN

UP

FOYER

LIVING ROOM

MAIN FLOOR

DECK

WIC

BEDROOM

DN

LINEN

BATH

MASTER BEDROOM

OPEN TO BELOW

Photography supplied by Alan Mascord Design Associates

4,768 sq. ft

- An impressive four-bedroom home, designed with imagination and style: ideal for formal entertaining or busy family life.

- A two-storyed ceiling and an awesome stone fireplace lend grandeur to a truly great room. The bank of windows allows enjoyment of all the seasons. A second cozy fireplace is found in the comfortable book-lined study.

- Elegant columns separate the formal dining room with its beautiful decorative ceiling, custom cabinetry and gleaming hardwood floors.

- The kitchen, with its island and peninsula counter, leads to a breakfast room that accesses both the rear porch and enclosed sunroom.

- The upper floor is as exciting as the main floor. A breathtaking master suite has its own fireplace and private deck and a magnificently appointed ensuite, which includes two very generous walk-in closets.

~ ROCKWOOD ~

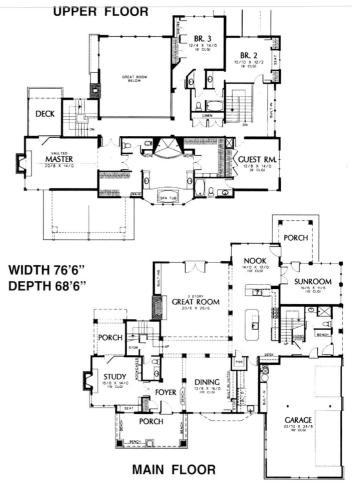

UPPER FLOOR

BR. 3
12/4 X 14/0
19' CLGI

BR. 2
12/10 X 12/2
19' CLGI

GREAT ROOM BELOW

DECK

LINEN

VAULTED MASTER
20/8 X 14/0

GUEST RM.
12/8 X 14/0
19' CLGI

SPA TUB

WIDTH 76'6"
DEPTH 68'6"

NOOK
14/0 X 12/0
(10' CLGI

SUNROOM
16/6 X 11/6
(10' CLGI

BENCH

2 STORY
GREAT ROOM
20/8 X 26/6

PORCH

PORCH

STOR

DESK

STUDY
15/0 X 14/0
(10' CLGI

DINING
13/8 X 16/0
(10' CLGI

GARAGE
22/10 X 34/8
(10' CLGI

FOYER

SEAT

PORCH

BENCH

MAIN FLOOR

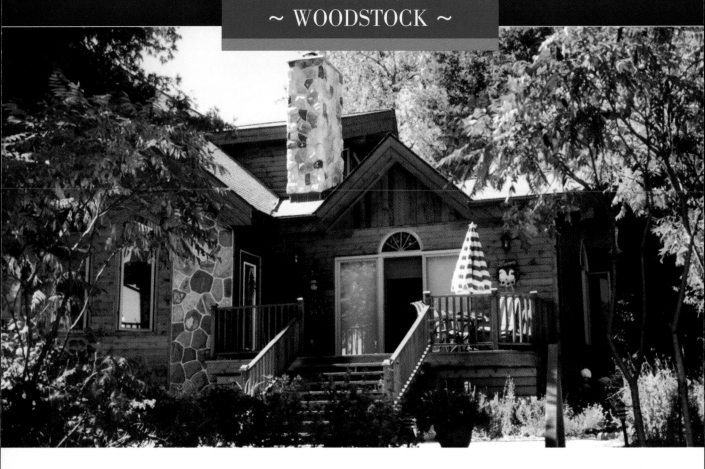

2,032 sq. ft

- This attractive home features a spacious entrance, two very private bedrooms, three bathrooms, laundry area and a marvellous kitchen.

- The master bedroom, with ensuite and huge walk-in closet, is situated in its own wing; the second bedroom with bath is located on the secluded upper level, with an adjacent loft open to the living areas below.

- The large sundeck is accessible from both the vaulted great room and the magnificent main floor master bedroom.

MAIN FLOOR

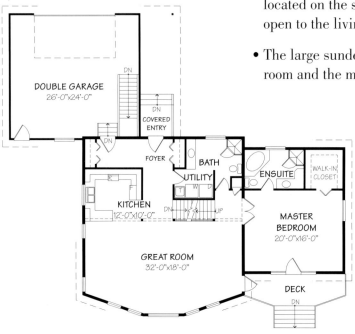

DOUBLE GARAGE
26'-0"x24'-0"

DN

DN
COVERED
ENTRY

DN

FOYER

BATH

UTILITY

ENSUITE

WALK-IN
CLOSET

KITCHEN
12'-0"x10'-0"

DN   UP

MASTER
BEDROOM
20'-0"x16'-0"

GREAT ROOM
32'-0"x18'-0"

DECK
DN

LOFT

BATH

BEDROOM
12'-0"x12'-0"

DN

OPEN TO BELOW

UPPER FLOOR

Photography supplied by The Meredith Corporation

4,454 sq. ft.

- This large and comfortable four-bedroom home offers an unusual but appealing floor plan. The main entry opens to a large sunroom that divides the home's living area from the private, main-floor master bedroom.

- The sunken living room has a fireplace with built-in bookcases and leads to a small, secluded library and to the formal dining room.

- The U-shaped kitchen with cook-top island and plentiful counter/cupboard space, is an epicure's delight. A multi-windowed breakfast nook and separate laundry room complete the kitchen area.

- The sizeable, airy upper floor offers three additional bedrooms, a loft and a unique full and half-bath combination. A balcony walkway leads to a large bonus room.

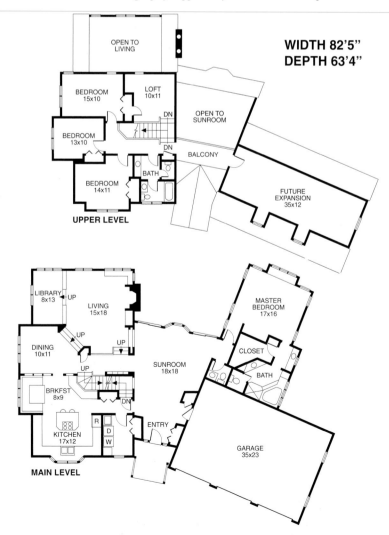

WIDTH 82'5"
DEPTH 63'4"

OPEN TO LIVING

BEDROOM 15x10

LOFT 10x11

DN

OPEN TO SUNROOM

BEDROOM 13x10

DN

BALCONY

BEDROOM 14x11

BATH

FUTURE EXPANSION 35x12

UPPER LEVEL

LIBRARY 8x13

UP

LIVING 15x18

MASTER BEDROOM 17x16

UP

UP

CLOSET

DINING 10x11

UP

SUNROOM 18x18

BATH

BRKFST 8x9

DN

KITCHEN 17x12

R
D
W

ENTRY

GARAGE 35x23

MAIN LEVEL

2,078 sq. ft.

- Unique roof lines and the use of glass add warmth and character to this elegant two-bedroom, chalet-style home.

- The enormous second-level master bedroom offers a large walk-in closet and full ensuite with separate shower.

- The main level features comfortable open-plan living and dining areas, a gourmet kitchen with exceptionally large island, the second bedroom, another full bath, and utility room with access to the garden.

~ BLACKCOMB ~

MAIN FLOOR

LAUNDRY

W   D

BATH

BEDROOM
16'-0"x16'-0"

LIN

F

KITCHEN
18'-0"x14'-0"

DW

PANTRY

OVEN

UP

DN

LIVING ROOM
18'-0"x18'-0"

DINING ROOM
18'-0"x14'-0"

OPTIONAL SUNDECK

UPPER FLOOR

MASTER
BEDROOM
18'-8"x22'-10"

BATH

W-I-C

DN

OPEN TO BELOW

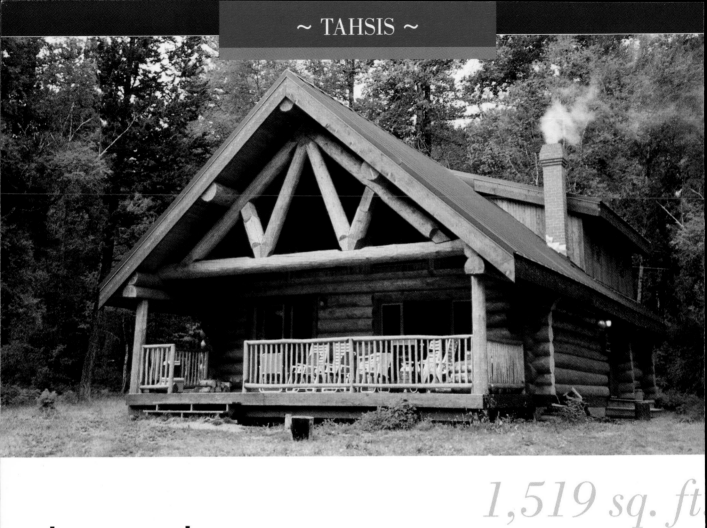

1,519 sq. ft.

MAIN FLOOR

- This log home offers the best in gracious living for the smaller family looking for great style. The great room with adjacent kitchen is perfect for family gatherings and entertaining.

- Double French doors off of the Great room doors bring the outdoors in, while a corner fireplace keeps the atmosphere warm and cozy.

- Upstairs features two private bedrooms, each with their own luxurious full bathrooms and large closets. This compact design features an abundance of simple pleasures.

UPPER FLOOR

,689 sq. ft.

- This magnificent three-bedroom home features dramatic vaulted ceilings over every bedroom.

- The master bedroom with full ensuite and walk-in closet is situated on the second level with a cheery loft.

- Natural light streams through the large clerestory windows between the split roof line and from the open design of the upper loft area over the sunroom.

MAIN FLOOR

KITCHEN
16'-0"x12'-0"

UTILITY

D

BATH

W

BEDROOM
14'-0"x10'-4"

SOLARIUM

DINING
16'-0"x12'-0"

BROOM

UP

BEDROOM
13'-6"x10'-0"

OPTIONAL DECK

LIVING ROOM
14'-0"x20'-0"

OPTIONAL DECK

UPPER FLOOR

BALCONY

BEDROOM
13'-6"x10'-0"

BATH

OPEN TO MAIN FLOOR

LOFT
10'-0"x12'-0"

WALK-IN CLOSET

DN

2,001 sq. ft

- Imagine waking up in the roomy master bedroom of this appealing, Victorian three-bedroom charmer, as light streams in through the romantic bay window. Two additional bedrooms, each with a huge closet, share a second full bathroom on the upper floor.

- On the main floor, the distinctive turret is enclosed by a pillared veranda—wonderful for those hot summer days. A separate rear deck is accessible from both the well-appointed kitchen and the living room.

- The living room boasts sloping, skylit ceilings and a cozy fireplace to warm up those cold and rainy winter evenings.

BEDROOM
10'-6"x11'-4"

BEDROOM
10'-8"x11'-6"

HALL

MASTER
BEDROOM
11'-0" x 21'-2"

BATH
1/2 WALL

ATTIC

SECOND FLOOR

DECK

1 1/2"CLG. REVEAL

LIVING ROOM
14'-0"x19'-4"

DINING
10'-6"x13'-4"

K.
11'-0"x12'-0"

FOYER

ISLAND

BREAKFAST
11'-0"x 9'-6"

LND.

PORCH

GARAGE
21'-4" x 21'-8"

STEP

WALK

56'-0"

FIRST FLOOR

43'-0"

2,152 sq. ft.

- This attractive three bedroom home features a sunken living room and spacious family room which offer an aura of comfort and warmth.

- The upper floor master bedroom is complete with ensuite and walk-in closet. The loft area is a wonderful space for working or just relaxing.

- Attached to the large kitchen is a laundry room, mud room and powder room.

UPPER FLOOR

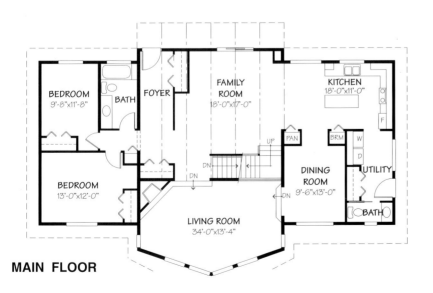

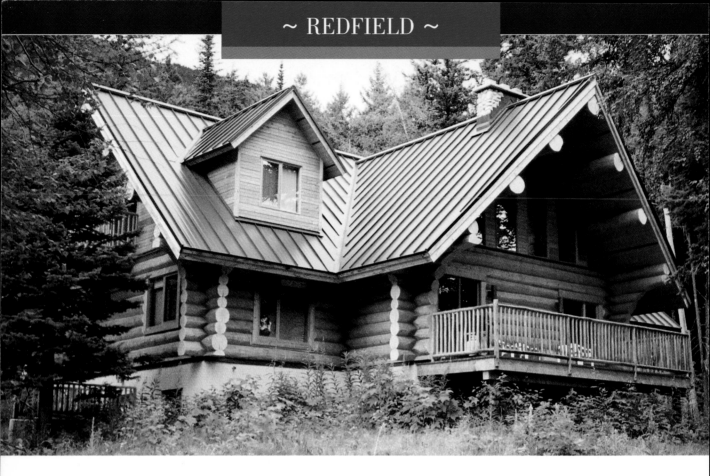

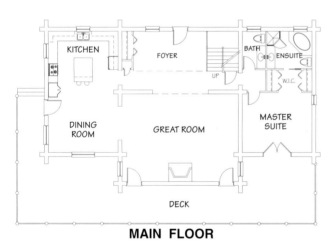

MAIN FLOOR

KITCHEN

FOYER

BATH

ENSUITE

UP

W.I.C.

DINING ROOM

GREAT ROOM

MASTER SUITE

DECK

2,629 sq. ft

• The appeal of this delightful design begins with gabled dormers on the second level and finishes with a beautiful yet functional layout with remarkable comfort. An impressive and welcoming foyer opens up to the bright and airy cathedral-ceiling great room, which highlights a floor to ceiling fireplace. Tucked away by the dining room is a generous gourmet kitchen with ample counter space.

• Upstairs, many charming features await, including an open-sided walkway which looks down onto the great room and foyer, a large master suite with a full en suite tucked into one of the dormers, and a cozy loft. Let your imagination soar when you personalize this adaptable design to fit your family's needs.

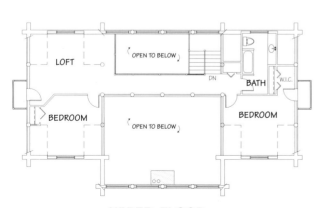

LOFT

OPEN TO BELOW

DN

BATH

W.I.C.

BEDROOM

OPEN TO BELOW

BEDROOM

UPPER FLOOR

1,589 sq. ft.

- This gorgeous home is designed for comfort, style and intimacy.

- The massive prow front takes full advantage of the outstanding view from this fine two-bedroom home and natural light permeates the vaulted living and dining areas.

- A separate wing features a huge master bedroom with ensuite and walk-in closet.

- Stonework on the walk-out basement and a pole railing system enhance the natural beauty of the cedar siding.

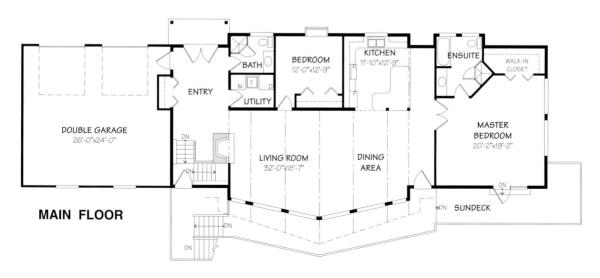

MAIN FLOOR

DOUBLE GARAGE
26'-0"x24'-0"

ENTRY

BATH

UTILITY

BEDROOM
12'-0"x12'-9"

KITCHEN
11'-10"x12'-9"

ENSUITE

WALK-IN CLOSET

LIVING ROOM
32'-0"x18'-7"

DINING AREA

MASTER BEDROOM
20'-2"x19'-2"

SUNDECK

Photography by John Ehrenclou

2,464 sq. ft.

- This stately Colonial four-bedroom home combines a traditional welcoming look with all the contemporary features one could want.

- A formal cross-hall living and dining room are bridged by a well-lit and spacious multi-storied foyer. The wrap-around porch adds a gracious hint of days gone by and leads to a large sundeck at the back of the house. This, in turn, becomes a screened-in porch area, which one can access from the sundeck and the breakfast room.

- Columns mark the Great Room with its porch access, built-in cabinetry and fireplace. A hallway with a powder room leads through the breakfast room to the sumptuously appointed kitchen. To facilitate formal entertaining, the kitchen opens to a walk-in pantry/laundry room, which then opens to the formal dining room.

- In addition to the balcony overlooking the foyer, the second floor boasts three spacious bedrooms sharing a full bath, and a superlative master suite, featuring a vaulted ceiling, well-appointed ensuite and its own private deck.

~ LOUISBURG ~

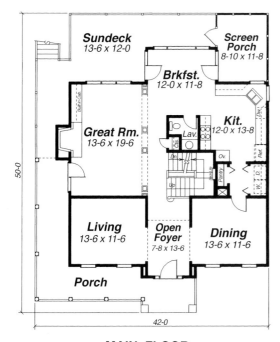

Sundeck
13-6 x 12-0

Screen Porch
8-10 x 11-8

Brkfst.
12-0 x 11-8

Kit.
12-0 x 13-8

Great Rm.
13-6 x 19-6

Lav.

Living
13-6 x 11-6

Open Foyer
7-8 x 13-6

Dining
13-6 x 11-6

Porch

50-0

42-0

MAIN FLOOR

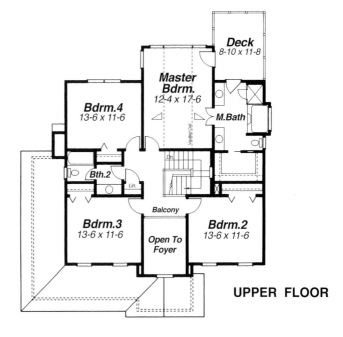

Deck
8-10 x 11-8

Master Bdrm.
12-4 x 17-6

M.Bath

Bdrm.4
13-6 x 11-6

Bth.2

Lin.

Dn.

Bdrm.3
13-6 x 11-6

Balcony

Open To Foyer

Bdrm.2
13-6 x 11-6

UPPER FLOOR

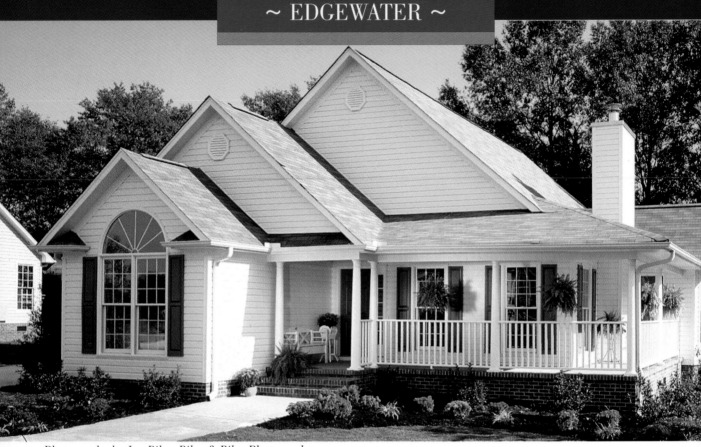

Photography by Jon Riley, Riley & Riley Photography

1,737 sq. ft.

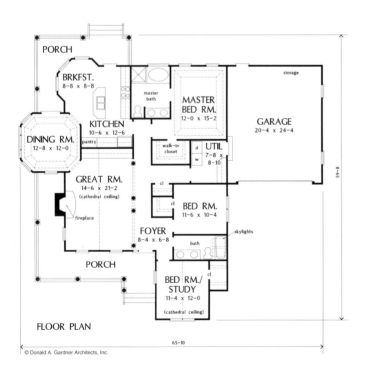

PORCH

BRKFST.
8-8 x 8-8

master
bath

MASTER
BED RM.
12-0 x 15-2

storage

GARAGE
20-4 x 24-4

KITCHEN
10-6 x 12-6

pantry

DINING RM.
12-8 x 12-0

walk-in
closet

d
w

UTIL
7-8 x
8-10

GREAT RM.
14-6 x 21-2
(cathedral ceiling)

cl

cl

BED RM.
11-6 x 10-4

fireplace

FOYER
8-4 x 6-8

skylights

bath

PORCH

cl

BED RM./
STUDY
11-4 x 12-0

(cathedral ceiling)

FLOOR PLAN

65-10

59-8

© Donald A. Gardner Architects, Inc.

- Charm, and a clever use of space and light, define this single level two-bedroom and den or three-bedroom home.

- The great room, with its majestic cathedral ceiling, gracious columns and cozy fireplace, has access to the wraparound porch as well as to the octagonal-shaped dining room.

- The breakfast bay has a similar shape and, with their multiple windows, these rooms truly bring the outdoors in. The generous kitchen has a centre island and a pantry.

- The spacious private master suite, with its tray ceiling, offers a well-appointed bath and large walk-in closet.

- The front bedroom, or study, has a cathedral ceiling and large circle-top window and shares the full bath with the third bedroom.

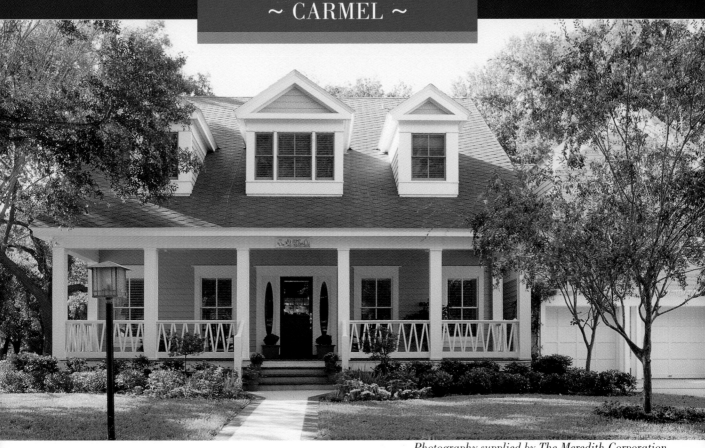

Photography supplied by The Meredith Corporation

4,292 sq. ft.

- The welcoming front porch and dormer windows create a cozy first impression which belies the size of this five-bedroom home.

- The main floor offers formal living and dining rooms which flank the foyer. The informal area is to the rear of the house and includes a large family room with two sets of French doors opening on to the porch, a bright breakfast nook, large kitchen, a mudroom and a playroom or nanny quarters with full bathroom attached.

- Upstairs via either of the two staircases, one finds a sumptuous master suite. The large bedroom has a bank of windows and leads to a dressing room with two generous closets and to the luxurious five-piece master ensuite. Each of the four additional bedrooms offer private access to one of two full bathrooms A large laundry/storage room completes the upper floor.

WIDTH 64'
DEPTH 65'

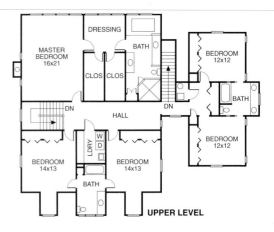

UPPER LEVEL

MAIN LEVEL

3,062 sq. ft.

- Truly a unique four-bedroom home. Numerous skylights and many windows make the surroundings a beautiful part of the home. The covered deck wraps around the house and leads down several sets of stairs to the water.

- The open plan main floor affords the finest in casual living. Gleaming hardwood floors, beautiful beams and wood ceilings give the home a very cozy feeling. The large stone fireplace invites curling up with a good book when the weather doesn't cooperate. The gourmet kitchen creates another focal point for family and friends.

- The upper floor boasts four large bedrooms. The master suite has an inviting fireplace which can be seen from either the bed, which also looks out at the water, or from the large soaker tub in the well-appointed ensuite. A beautiful wooden spiral staircase leads to the private den or office.

MAIN FLOOR

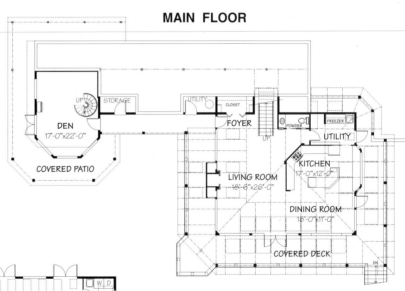

DEN
17'-0"x22'-0"

STORAGE

UTILITY

CLOSET

FOYER

POWDER

FREEZER

UTILITY

KITCHEN
17'-0"x12'-0"

LIVING ROOM
18'-6"x26'-0"

DINING ROOM
18'-0"x11'-0"

COVERED PATIO

COVERED DECK

SUNDECK

WALK IN CLOSET

ENS

MASTER BEDROOM
19'-0"x17'-0"

BEDROOM
12'-0"x13'-8"

BEDROOM
12'-0"x13'-8"

BEDROOM
12'-0"x13'-8"

LINEN

W D

LAUNDRY

BATH

COVERED DECK

UPPER FLOOR

Photography by Jon Riley, Riley & Riley Photography

1,655 sq. ft.

c 1996 Donald A Gardner Architects, Inc.

- A recessed front porch and two charming gables add to the curb appeal of this compact three-bedroom home.

- Interior columns dramatically open to the kitchen/breakfast room and to the great room, which boasts an impressive cathedral ceiling and a fireplace.

- The master suite is completely self-contained in its own wing at the back of the house. The tray ceiling of the bedroom, two large windows and lovely french doors, which open on to the large rear deck with spa, ensure a light, airy feeling. This continues into the five-piece ensuite, where the sunlight streams through skylights.

1,841 sq. ft.

- The appealing design of this stately three-bedroom home offers privacy and lifestyle.

- The large island kitchen, utility, bath, and vaulted living and dining areas, are located on the main floor, as is the secluded master bedroom, with enormous walk-in closet and access to the adjoining screen room.

- Two more bedrooms, and a full bath are set in the upper level, with an expansive loft that overlooks the prow windows in the living areas.

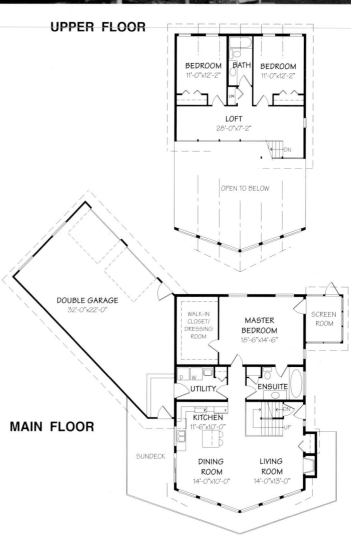

UPPER FLOOR

BEDROOM
11'-0"x12'-2"

BATH

BEDROOM
11'-0"x12'-2"

LIN

LOFT
28'-0"x7'-2"

DN

OPEN TO BELOW

MAIN FLOOR

DOUBLE GARAGE
32'-0"x22'-0"

WALK-IN CLOSET/ DRESSING ROOM

MASTER BEDROOM
18'-6"x14'-6"

SCREEN ROOM

D | W

UTILITY

ENSUITE

KITCHEN
11'-6"x10'-0"

UP

DN

SUNDECK

DINING ROOM
14'-0"x10'-0"

LIVING ROOM
14'-0"x13'-0"

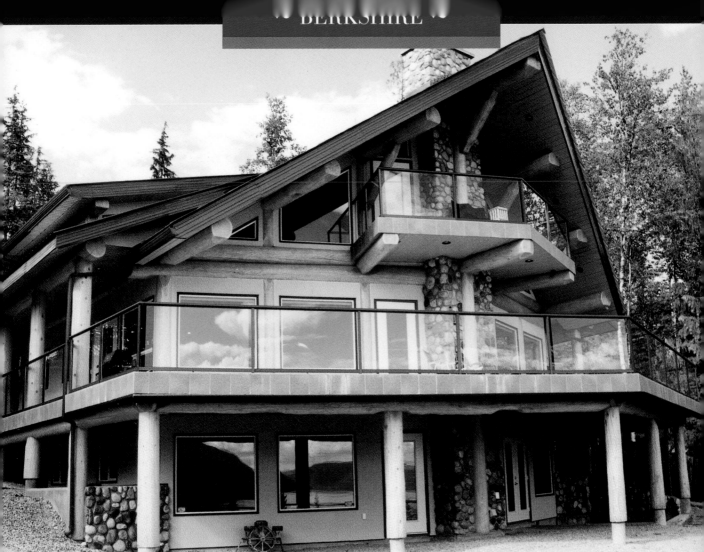

2,654 sq. ft

- The ultimate retreat or vacation log home. Watch spectacular sunsets from the expansive decks on both levels.

- Entertaining is a joy in the impressive open plan great room and dining room. The lovely spacious kitchen has an island work station with all the amenities for creating memorable meals.

- The luxurious master bedroom is this home's most unique design feature with its catwalk over the great room.

- A huge games room is conveniently situated above the double garage.

~ BERKSHIRE ~

MAIN FLOOR

PWDR
DEN
UP
DECK
LIVING ROOM
DOUBLE GARAGE
UP
DN
MUD ROOM
COVERED WALKWAY
DINING ROOM
KITCHEN
COVERED DECK

UPPER FLOOR

ENSUITE
GAMES ROOM
DN
OPEN TO BELOW
STORAGE
DN
CATWALK
MASTER BEDROOM
BALCONY
OPEN TO BELOW
WIC

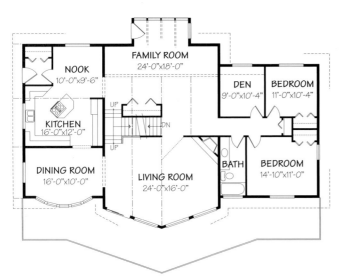

MAIN FLOOR

2,880 sq. ft

- This handsome three-bedroom (plus den) home with family room offers ample space for everyone to enjoy their own privacy.

- On the second level is the totally private master bedroom, with full ensuite, and a cozy loft that opens on to the living areas below.

- The huge sundeck extends the generous indoor living areas, which include breathtaking prow windows and a sunny breakfast nook.

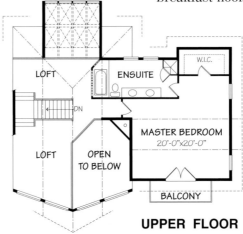

UPPER FLOOR

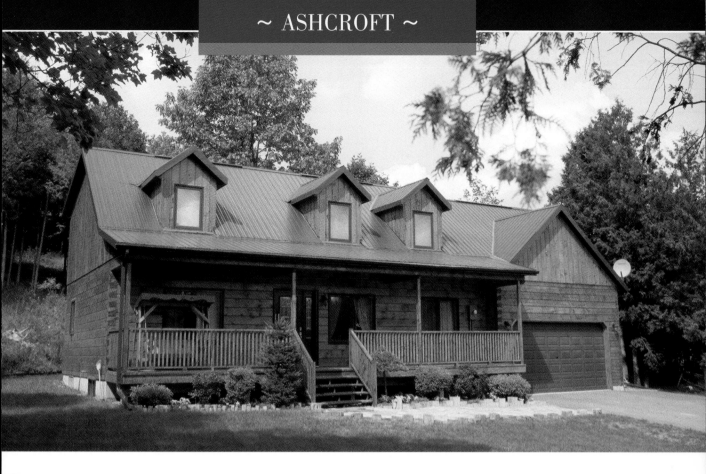

1,752 sq. ft.

- This luxurious three-bedroom log home has the added appeal of a covered front porch and a covered deck at the rear. The large, bright kitchen features an L-shaped island and opens to both the living room, with its cozy fireplace, and to the dining room.

- Two bedrooms or a bedroom and den share a full bathroom on one side of the house.

- Upstairs, the master suite also boasts a private loft area to allow for some space away from the family, or room to curl up with a good book.

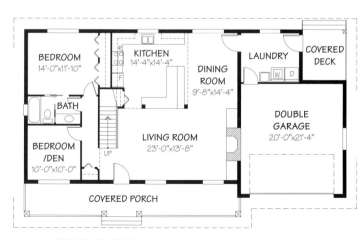

MAIN FLOOR

BEDROOM
14'-0"x11'-10"

KITCHEN
14'-4"x14'-4"

DINING ROOM
9'-8"x14'-4"

LAUNDRY

COVERED DECK

BATH

LIVING ROOM
23'-0"x13'-8"

DOUBLE GARAGE
20'-0"x21'-4"

BEDROOM /DEN
10'-0"x10'-0"

UP

COVERED PORCH

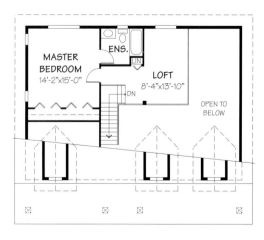

UPPER FLOOR

MASTER BEDROOM
14'-2"x15'-0"

ENS.

LIN

LOFT
8'-4"x13'-10"

DN

OPEN TO BELOW

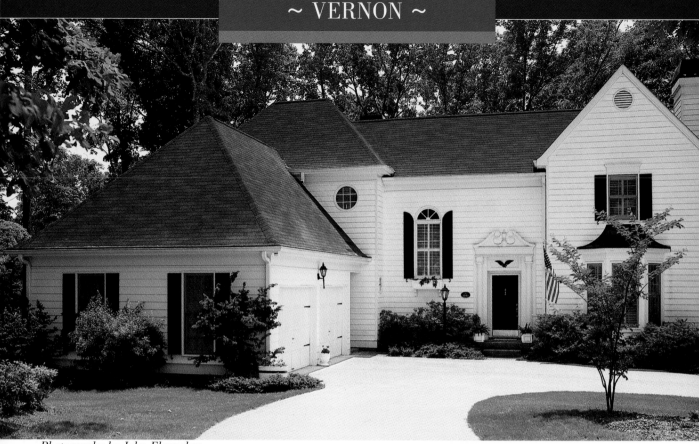

Photography by John Ehrenclou

61'-1"

58'-0"

Morning Rm
13-5 x 18-0

Flue

Corner Fireplace

UP

Dining Rm
13-3 x 13-8

Deck

Screened Porch
14-10 x 11-9

Built-In Book Case

Kitchen
17-3 x 11-5

Island

Pantry

Oven

Ref.

Pwdr.

Storage

Foyer

UP

Living Rm
14-9 x 19-5

Books

F. W

Optional Mechanical Placement

First Floor

Garage
21-5 x 25-8

Br #3
13-5 x 12-0

Planter

W.P. Tub

Mstr. Bath

Trey Clg

Mstr. Br
14-9 x 15-8
Flat @ 13'-0"

Foyer
12-3 x 12-3
Flat @ 4'-4"

Hall

DN

Liner

Br #2
15-1 x 11-1

Util

DN

Open to Below

Sitting Rm
14-9 x 9-5

Walk-In-Closet

Second Floor

Bonus Rm
11-5 x 20-8
Flat @ 8'-0"

Crawl Space Access

Slab/Crawl Space Option

3,065 sq. ft.

- This attractive, three-bedroom home has immediate appeal with its large windows and distinctive shutters. The spacious bay-windowed living room, with its fireplace and built-in bookcase, opens to a screened porch and deck.

- The large kitchen with its pantry, island, built-in desk and ample cupboard space, adjoins a comfortable morning room which features a bay window and corner fireplace. A second staircase leads from the morning room to the upper floor. Across the hall from the formal dining room is a half bath and a large storage area.

- Upstairs, the impressive master suite features an entry foyer, separate sitting room, huge walk-in closet and lavish bathroom, complete with whirlpool tub, separate shower stall and two vanities. Two additional bedrooms, with private access to a full bath, a laundry/utility room and a bonus area above the garage complete the upper floor.

2,429 sq. ft.

- From the moment you enter this log home, you'll know you are somewhere special. A large foyer welcomes you into the home, while a light-filled great room tantalizes your senses. The central fireplace is a natural divider that doesn't interfere with the sense of openness. Many doors lead out to the full wrap-around deck, truly bringing the outdoors in.

- The spacious upper level features 3 large bedrooms, two complete bathrooms and plenty of charming dormer windows to let the light flood in. This extraordinary home combines the rustic charm of traditional log home living with the modern conveniences of formal entertaining

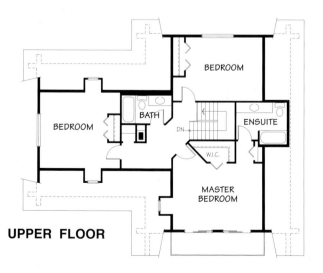

UPPER FLOOR

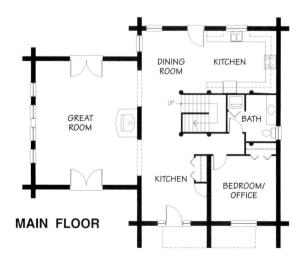

MAIN FLOOR

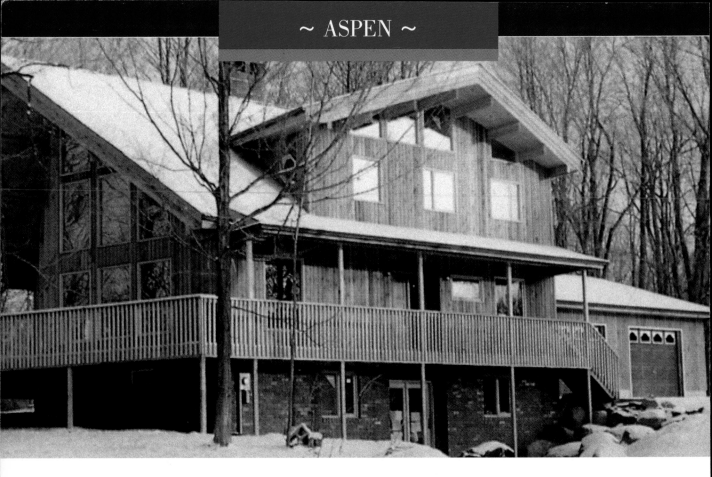

2,069 sq. ft.

- This is leisure living at its best. The stately glass prow front of this gorgeous three-bedroom home provides a bright, airy atmosphere in both the living and dining rooms.

- The upper floor has two large bedrooms and full bath, along with a large sitting area open to the main floor.

- The front wraparound balcony is ideal for outdoor entertaining.

GARAGE
24'-0"x16'-0"

BROOM

D
W
UTILITY

BEDROOM
12'-0"x13'-0"

BATH

DN

KITCHEN
14'-0"x9'-0"

PANTRY

UP

DINING ROOM
12'-0"x16'-0"

LIVING ROOM
20'-0"x18'-0"

SUNDECK

MAIN FLOOR

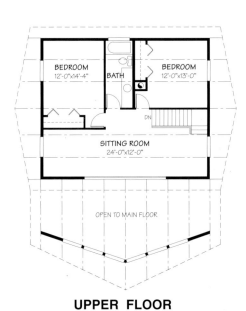

BEDROOM
12'-0"x14'-4"

BATH

BEDROOM
12'-0"x13'-0"

DN

SITTING ROOM
24'-0"x12'-0"

OPEN TO MAIN FLOOR

UPPER FLOOR

Photography by John Ehrenclou

3,903 sq. ft.

- This impressive four-bedroom family home is characterized by the Great Room, featuring a massive fireplace, built-in bookshelves and access to the cozy loft study. The large country kitchen area, with its cooktop island and many other amenities, adjoins both the dining room and a spacious laundry/utility room.

- Also on the main floor is the master suite with private deck, built-in bookcases, two walk-in closets and ensuite bathroom with separate shower stall and skylit bathtub. A secondary bedroom on this floor accesses a full bathroom across the hall.

- The lower floor provides two generous bedrooms that share a full bathroom. A spacious recreation room with cozy fireplace and bar area opens to the downstairs patio.

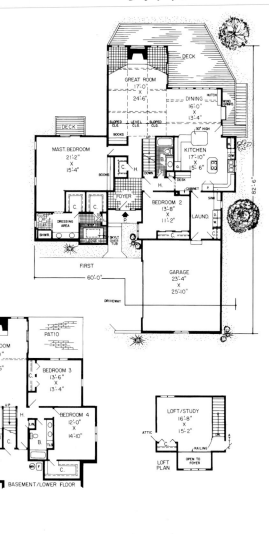

Photography by Glenn Graves

2,563 sq. ft

- The front porch offers an immediate welcome to all who enter this four-bedroom country classic. A central hallway links the formal dining room, with its bay window overlooking the porch, and the gourmet kitchen and adjoining hearth room at the rear of the house.

- The high-ceilinged living room, with its many windows, shares an impressive two-way fireplace with the cozy hearth room. The rear deck can be accessed from both these rooms and is an ideal spot for informal dining.

- The private master suite is also on the main floor and adjoins a luxurious ensuite bathroom with separate shower stall, his and her vanities and a generous walk-in closet.

- The upper floor features a balcony overlooking the activities of the downstairs living room. Three additional bedrooms share two bathrooms. This floor also has a multitude of storage space.

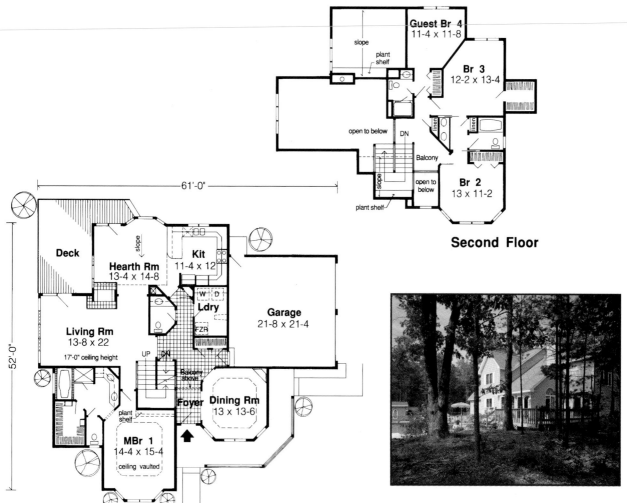

Second Floor

Guest Br 4
11-4 x 11-8

Br 3
12-2 x 13-4

Br 2
13 x 11-2

slope

plant shelf

open to below

DN

Balcony

open to below

plant shelf

linen

linen

slope

First Floor

61'-0"

52'-0"

Deck

Hearth Rm
13-4 x 14-8

Kit
11-4 x 12

slope

Living Rm
13-8 x 22

17'-0" ceiling height

W D

Ldry

FZR

Garage
21-8 x 21-4

UP DN

Balcony above

Foyer

Dining Rm
13 x 13-6

plant shelf

MBr 1
14-4 x 15-4

ceiling vaulted

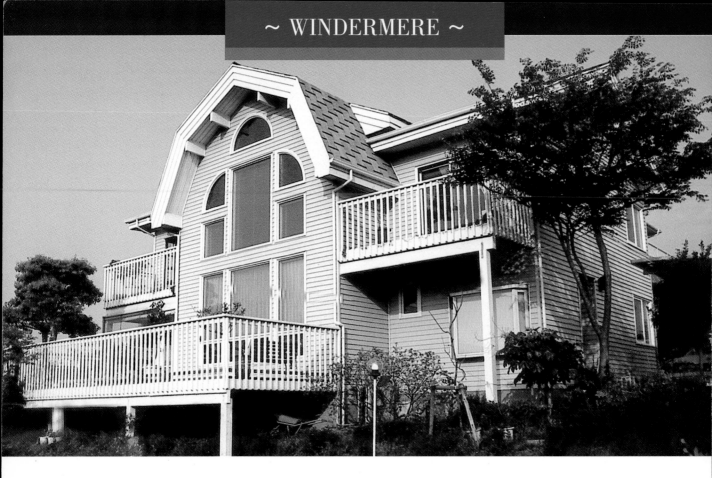

1,970 sq. ft

- The charm of this unique three bedroom home (plus study) is highlighted by two enormous upper-floor bedroom suites, each with a large ensuite and private sundeck.

- This majestic home has windows galore to take advantage of the spectacular view. An interesting portico leads into the spacious foyer and sunken great room.

- Sundecks add to the outdoor living enjoyment of this outstanding house.

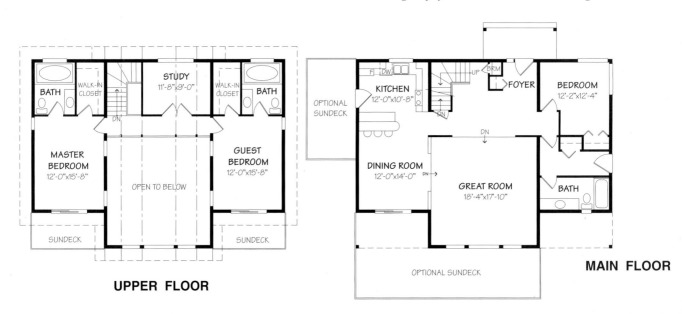

UPPER FLOOR

BATH · WALK-IN CLOSET · STUDY 11'-8"x9'-0" · WALK-IN CLOSET · BATH

MASTER BEDROOM 12'-0"x15'-8" · OPEN TO BELOW · GUEST BEDROOM 12'-0"x15'-8"

SUNDECK · SUNDECK

DN

MAIN FLOOR

OPTIONAL SUNDECK

F DW · KITCHEN 12'-0"x10'-8" · UP · BRM · FOYER · BEDROOM 12'-2"x12'-4"

DN

DINING ROOM 12'-0"x14'-0" · DN · GREAT ROOM 18'-4"x17'-10" · BATH

OPTIONAL SUNDECK

1,262 sq. ft.

- The vaulted living area and kitchen act as the hub of this open-plan bungalow, with natural light streaming in through the splendid solarium and the majestic windows.

- Each of the two bedrooms is situated in a separate wing for maximum privacy, and the master bedroom features magnificent prow windows.

- A utility room and a full bath on the main level round out the elegant floor plan. Log siding adds to the visual appeal of this practical and appealing home.

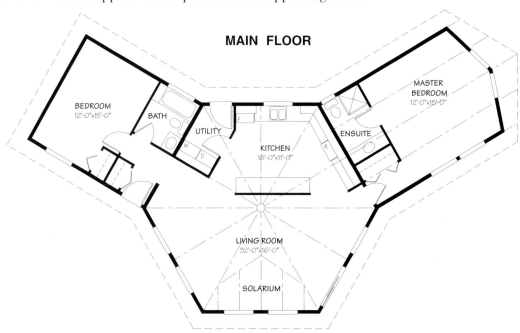

MAIN FLOOR

BEDROOM
12'-0"x15'-0"

BATH

UTILITY

MASTER
BEDROOM
12'-0"x15'-0"

ENSUITE

KITCHEN
18'-0"x11'-0"

LIVING ROOM
32'-0"x16'-0"

SOLARIUM

Photography supplied by Larry E. Belk

3,109 sq. ft

- Twin arches give a distinctive European look to this attractive four-bedroom home, while the clever floor plan provides for all the demands of a modern lifestyle. The two-story foyer and living room, with its twin doors opening to the rear deck, give a spacious feeling to the main floor and, with the adjoining dining room, provide an excellent area for formal entertaining.

- The efficiently-designed kitchen, with its pantry and angled work area, opens into a bay-windowed breakfast room and the spacious family room with its fireplace and rear porch access.

- The private master suite occupies one wing of the main floor and includes a luxury ensuite complete with a corner whirlpool tub, separate shower stall and two walk-in closets.

- The upper floor has three bedrooms, two full bathrooms and a games room. Additional space over the garage is also available.

WIDTH 64'6"
DEPTH 55'10"

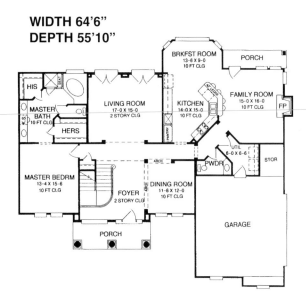

BRKFST ROOM
13-6 X 9-0
10 FT CLG

PORCH

HIS

MASTER
BATH
10 FT CLG

LIVING ROOM
17-0 X 15-0
2 STORY CLG

KITCHEN
14-0 X 15-0
10 FT CLG

FAMILY ROOM
15-0 X 16-0
10 FT CLG

FP

HERS

PANTRY

MASTER BEDRM
13-4 X 15-6
10 FT CLG

FOYER
2 STORY CLG

DINING ROOM
11-6 X 12-0
10 FT CLG

PWDR

UTIL
6-0 X 6-6

STOR

ARCH

GARAGE

PORCH

FIRST FLOOR

BEDROOM 3
13-8 X 12-0

ATTIC

OPEN TO LIVING ROOM BELOW

BATH 2

GAME ROOM
14-6 X 16-4

LIN

DRESSING

BATH
3

BEDROOM 2
13-8 X 12-0

OPEN TO
FOYER
BELOW

BEDROOM 4
11-6 X 12-4

DRESSING

EXPANDABLE AREA
13-0 X 22-0

SECOND FLOOR

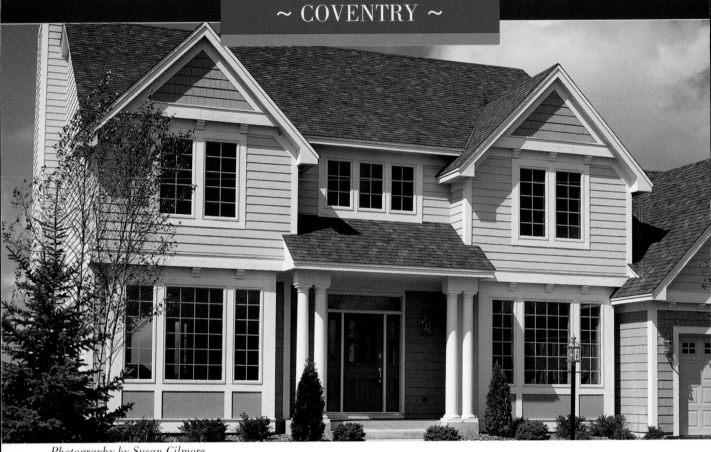

Photography by Susan Gilmore

2,432 sq. ft.

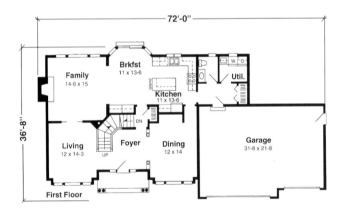

First Floor

72'-0"

36'-8"

Family
14-6 x 15

Brkfst
11 x 13-6

Kitchen
11 x 13-6

Util.

W D

Living
12 x 14-3

Foyer

Dining
12 x 14

Garage
31-8 x 21-8

UP
DN

Second Floor

Mstr Br
15-6 x 17

w.p. tub

dressing
linen

Br 2
12 x 13-3

Open

Br 3
11-9 x 12-3

DN

- The entrance to this stylish three-bedroom home is sheltered by an attractive columned porch. The two-story foyer gives access to the formal, large-windowed living and dining rooms.

- The gourmet kitchen, with its island and pantry, opens into a multi-windowed breakfast room and to the comfortable family room, which features large windows and a fireplace. A half bathroom and large laundry/utility room and an additional storage area complete the main floor.

- The stairway to the upper floor leads to a spacious hallway. The huge master suite encompasses the rear part of the house, and adjoins a dressing area and exceptionally large walk-in closet, leading to a luxurious ensuite bathroom with whirlpool tub, separate shower and dual vanities. Two front facing additional bedrooms share a full bathroom.

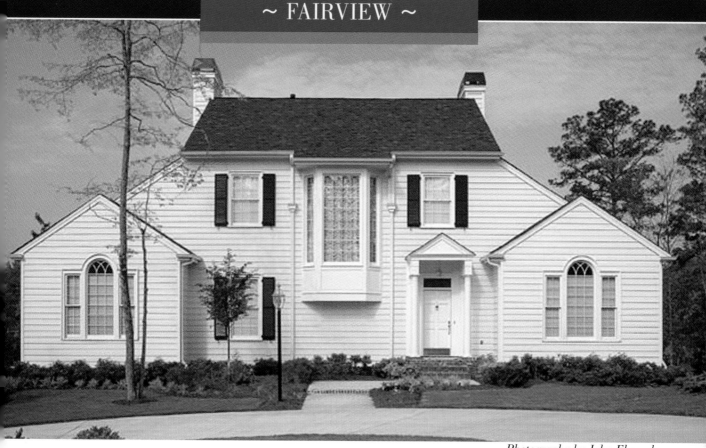

Photography by John Ehrenclou

4,091 sq. ft.

- An eye-catching feature of this unique traditional home is the large bay window illuminating the stairwell to the second floor. The entry foyer opens directly to an impressive great room which is ideal for entertaining.

- The dining and living rooms are separated by a large and efficient kitchen. Two secondary bedrooms, each with its own bathroom, are located on the left wing of the main floor.

- An enormous master suite fills the entire upper floor. This is highlighted by an exposed beam ceiling, a cozy fireplace and a generous walk-in closet.

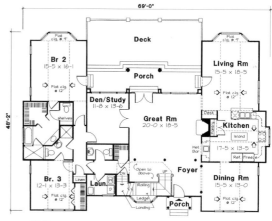

FIRST FLOOR PLAN

SECOND FLOOR

1,157 sq. ft.

- This charming cottage has great appeal in any location. The living space is enhanced by the large porch which allows outdoor living while still affording protection from the elements.

- The warmth and comfort of wood: floor, ceiling and bannisters, set the tone inside. French doors frame both sides of the wood-burning fireplace. Every part of the cabin, from the efficiently designed kitchen to the sunlit bedroom, is designed to take advantage of the view.

- Upstairs a large open plan loft area, with many skylights, affords complete flexibility. A second bedroom and den, children's play area, or the ability to accommodate many visitors.

~ CALICO ~

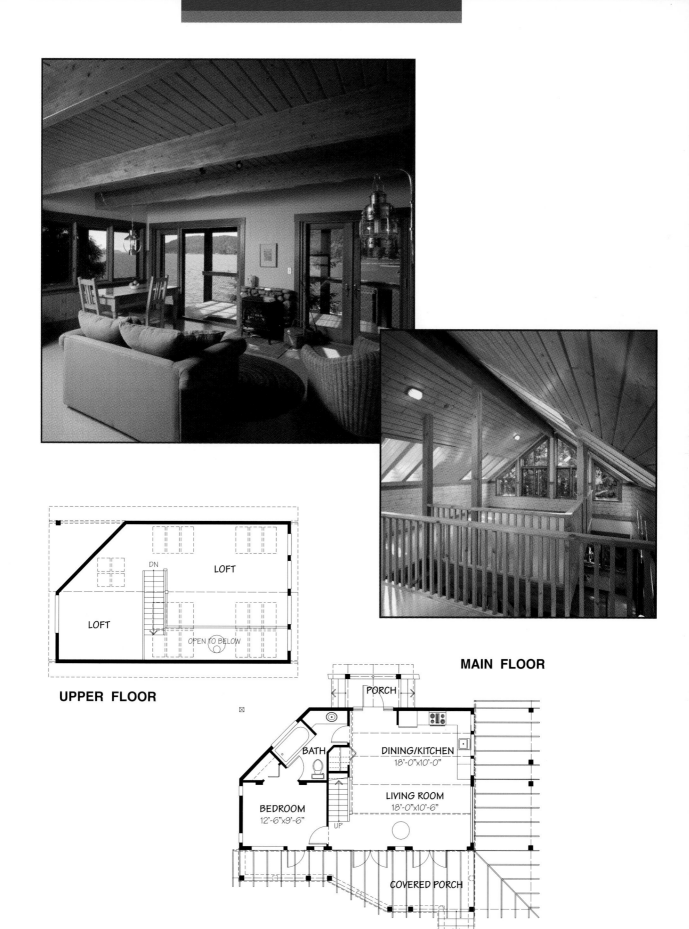

UPPER FLOOR

LOFT

DN

LOFT

OPEN TO BELOW

MAIN FLOOR

PORCH

BATH

DINING/KITCHEN
18'-0"x10'-0"

BEDROOM
12'-6"x9'-6"

LIVING ROOM
18'-0"x10'-6"

UP

COVERED PORCH

1,617 sq. ft

- This magnificent three-bedroom home is designed to harmonize with its surroundings. The great room offers a beautiful prow front, overlooking the large deck.

- The large kitchen, with its island stovetop, features three large windows overlooking another part of the garden. A breakfast solarium further enhances the feeling that the outdoors is part of the living space.

- The upper floor contains the generous master suite, skylit by the solarium, which it overlooks. A deck, accessed by French doors, offers a private retreat. A soaker tub with corner windows provides a focal point in the ensuite bathroom.

UPPER FLOOR

BALCONY

MASTER BEDROOM
13'-5"x20'-0"

ENS.

OPEN TO BELOW

DN

OPEN TO BELOW

KITCHEN
19'-6"x16'-0"

O/MW

FOYER

F

BEDROOM
12'-10"x9'-8"

BREAKFAST
6'-0"x12'-6"

DINING ROOM

UP

LIN

BATH

BEDROOM
13'-8"x9'-8"

GREAT ROOM
20'-0"x15'-0"

DECK

MAIN FLOOR

Photography supplied by Alan Mascord Design Associa

2,328 sq. ft

◄57'-2"►

58'-7"

NOOK
8/0 X 15/0

FAMILY
15/0 X 13/4
(9' CLG)

DINING
13/0 X 10/0

LIVING
13/0 X 12/4

GARAGE
23/0 X 21/4

First floor

- Decorative window inserts , attractive siding and the use of large windows add to the curb appeal of this four-bedroom home. A welcoming covered porch opens on to a large foyer. The open living area is ideal for entertaining.

- The rear of the home contains a large kitchen with island range and sunny breakfast nook, which flows into the spacious family room with its corner fireplace. A powder room and a laundry room complete the main floor layout.

- The upstairs master suite has a beautiful alcove for a soaker tub, as well as a large walk-in closet. Three additional bedrooms share a second full bathroom.

MASTER
12/8 X 16/0

BR. 2
10/0 X 12/0

BR. 3
13/0 X 11/0

BR. 4
10/8 X 10/0

PLANT SHELF

Second floor

,450 sq. ft.

- Get back to the basics with this charming log design. Enjoy the expansive open-living concept of this dwelling. A large gourmet kitchen is conveniently located within the spacious, light-filled great room, making this the ideal home for entertaining.

- A bedroom/office, full bath and complete laundry facilities round off the main floor, while an impressive master bedroom with full en suite is secluded in the privacy of the second level. This home features large walls of glass and ample wrap-around deck space, so whether you are inside or out, you will always be treated to a spectacular view

UPPER FLOOR

MAIN FLOOR

Photography supplied by Design Basic

2,090 sq. ft

MAIN FLOOR

38'-0"

48'-0"

Bfst. 11x13
Kit. 9x14
Grt. rm. 18x14
DESK
DN UP
SHELVES
R.
P.
Dn. 12x11
WRAP-AROUND PORCH
Gar. 20x22

SECOND FLOOR

Br. 12x10
Mbr. 15x13
DN
D. W.
Br. 11x11
Br. 11x11
LIN.
WHIRL POOL

• A wrap-around porch highlights this four-bedroom country style home. Off the foyer, the dining room overlooks the porch and leads to the well-equipped kitchen with its pantry and island . The light filled breakfast room, with built-in desk, completes the kitchen area.

• The expansive Great Room is accented by large windows and an impressive fireplace. An additional window on the landing enhances the light quality of this room.

• Double doors on the upstairs landing lead to the private master suite with its luxury ensuite and impressive closet space. Three other bedrooms share a full bathroom on this floor, with a laundry room conveniently located down the hall.

Photography supplied by Bob Shimet, Hedrich Blessing Studios

2,450 sq. ft.

- This four-bedroom ranch house offers a generous floor plan. Off the foyer, a large library or den, with built-in bookshelves, shares a two-way fireplace with the adjacent living room. Next to the library is a small, semi-private alcove, ideal for those quiet moments.

- The large kitchen featuring a central island, pantry and built-in china cupboards, is separated from the dining area by an angled cooktop peninsula. Doors from the dinning area and the living room lead to the screen porch and the large rear deck.

- The comfortable master suite has a corner firer place, and a large skylit ensuite with shower, whirlpool tub and walk-in closet. Three additional bedrooms share a full bathroom.

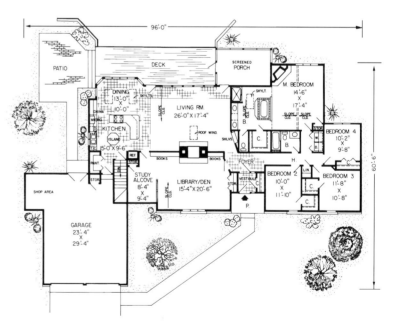

MAIN FLOOR

UPPER FLOOR

1,872 sq. ft.

- The distinctive gazebo at the end of the rear deck enhances the covered porches of this charming three-bedroom home. A high ceilinged entry foyer separates a well-equipped kitchen, with plentiful counter space and separate pantry, from the combined laundry/bathroom.

- A fireplace highlights a very spacious living room at the rear of the house, which opens to the dining room. Both rooms access the rear deck.

- One side of the upper floor is taken up by the master suite with its luxurious ensuite and enormous walk-in closet. A galleried hallway, open to the downstairs entry foyer, leads to the two secondary bedrooms.

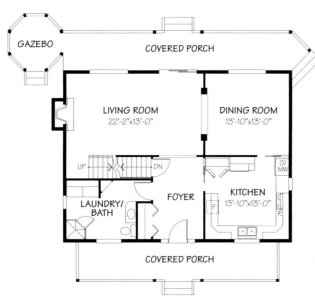

MAIN FLOOR

Photography supplied by Studer Design

2,354 sq. ft.

- The columned front porch of this enchanting three-bedroom home leads to a spacious entry foyer which offers gracious access to the impressive great room, formal dining room and large kitchen.

- The gourmet kitchen features a walk-in pantry, island working area and a pass-through to the dining room. It also opens into an expansive breakfast and sitting area with many windows, a built-in entertainment centre and access to the rear porch. A computer room, full bathroom and laundry room complete the main floor.

- In addition to the two guest bedrooms, full bath, ample closet space, and a balcony open to the lower floor, the upper floor presents a generous master bedroom with huge ensuite and walk-in closet. The sloped ceiling of the master bedroom adds distinction to this large and comfortable room.

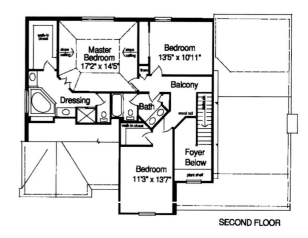

SECOND FLOOR

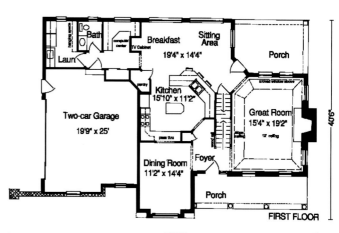

FIRST FLOOR

The Quality of Light

Windows, skylights and solariums are usually the first architectural details to attract our attention in a stunning house exterior. They're also the first things we notice when we walk into a room. Windows and skylights infuse our homes with natural light, an open and airy feeling of spaciousness and comfort. Sunrooms and solariums bring the beautiful outdoors into our homes, while protecting us from inclement weather.

Linwood Homes offers a huge range of windows, skylights and solariums to suit all styles of houses. You can enhance any plan with the generous use of natural light.

Once you have selected your ideal plan and customized it in consultation with your Linwood design representative, you can now design your finished living spaces. You have the wonderful opportunity to create a distinctive interior as unique as you are! As Linwood's Interior division, **Maple Homes** provides a custom package that can include interior design and selected finishing materials. Since 1989, we have offered a wide range of top quality materials that can be delivered direct to your building site. This proven system comes complete with full technical support and dependable service. You can combine this flexible interior package with a Linwood post and beam, log or conventional home package for practically everything you need to build your dream home.

- **Wood Flooring**
  Prefinished flooring with 10 coats of UV cured urethane with an aluminum oxide coating guaranteed to last. Strip and parquet available in hard maple, red oak, birch, and cherry. Unfinished maple, oak, fir and pine flooring are also available.

- **Wood Molding**
  Standard and custom profiles of baseboard, casing, crown and chairrails available in primed, hemlock, fir, oak and maple.

- **Kitchen Cabinetry**
  Kitchens, vanities, china cabinets, bookcases and wall units are all possible with our quality line of cabinets. A multitude of door styles are available in painted, oak, maple, cherry and fir. Design is included.

- **Interior Doors**
  Solid cedar, fir, pine, oak and maple in many sizes and designs. Prehung in jambs with hardware.

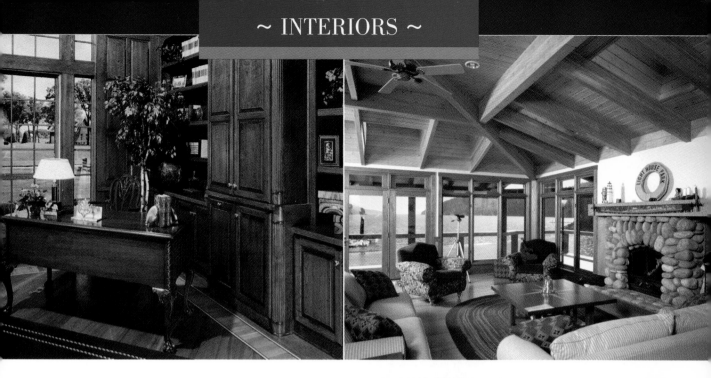

- **Cedar Garage Doors**
  All Cedar garage doors in many sizes and designs.

- **Stairs**
  Parts or premade stair units in hemlock, oak or maple. Custom curved units.

- **Wood Stove or Fireplace**
  Pedestal or insert stoves and energy efficient fireplaces in wood burning or gas.

- **Plumbing Fixtures**
  Sinks, bathtubs, jet tubs, faucets and showers.

- **Hot Tubs**
  Deluxe 2 ~ 8 person spas with up to 45 jets, ozone, whisper-flo and other options in a red cedar cabinet.

MAPLE HOMES
CANADA

Maple Homes provides you with a wide range of choices, quality and convenience at an affordable price. We will work closely with you to find the best interior finishing products to complement your design, concept and budget.

All you have to do is call: **1-800-663-5693** or, visit our website: **www.maplehomes.com/interior**

How To Proceed

We hope you have enjoyed this outstanding selection of designer homes and are inspired by the ideas you have seen. Nothing could be more simple than to explore your dream further. There is no obligation and no cost when you contact us.

Choose a Design

This is one of the most comprehensive collections of high quality homes ever published and available for sale. These are not line drawings but real homes crafted with great attention to detail and built with pride. Initially, all you have to do is select the name of the design(s) in which you are interested. This design can be fully customized at a later stage to suit your own specific needs should you so desire.

Contact Us at Garlinghouse

the Garlinghouse company

HELPING TO BUILD DREAMS
SINCE 1907

USA and Canada call toll free at 1-800-235-5700
or fax to 1-860-659-5692
All foreign residents call 1-860-659-5667
Monday to Friday 8:00 am to 8:00 pm
Eastern Standard Time.

The operator will take your name and contact information, including the design in which you are interested, where you live and where you intend to build.

Alternatively, you can simply fill in the attached information sheet and send it to:

The Live Your Dream Collection   Source Code: H1TD2

Garlinghouse Company
174 Oakwood Drive
Glastonbury, CT 06033

NAME: _____

STREET: _____

CITY: _____

STATE/PROVINCE: _____ ZIP/POSTAL CODE: _____

DAYTIME PHONE NUMBER: _____

E-MAIL: _____

NAME OF DESIGN: _____

_____

LOCATION OF BUILDING LOT: _____

ESTIMATED CONSTRUCTION DATE: _____

Expert Assistance from Linwood

Within 48 hours of receiving your call or written information sheet, you will be contacted by your nearest Linwood representative. They will provide you with full details of the standard features contained in the home package you have selected, as well as the package cost. If required, the representative will also help you fully customize the house to suit your needs, and assist you in determining any design changes. These changes may be as extensive as you wish.

Additionally, your representative will assist you in calculating the cost of all the other components of your new home, together with tips and advice on how to deal with contractors and obtain building permits. If you do not have your own contractor they will help you to find a reliable and competent team to build your dream.

LINWOOD
custom homes

Order Your Home Package

Only when you have finalized your design and are satisfied with the corresponding package price, will you be asked to sign a purchase order. At this stage you will need to make a down payment to commence the production process. You will then receive construction blueprints meeting the building and code standards for your intended location. The building materials will be shipped when and where you want them, together with a detailed construction manual. You may also contact the factory at any time for further assistance.

Building a custom designed home has never been this easy!

Important Information to Remember:

- You are purchasing a home package based on the architectural design you have selected.

- This design can be fully customized to meet your exact requirements.

- The home package contains the materials required to construct and finish the exterior of your home with the exception of the concrete foundation and stonework.

- The construction blueprints will conform to local building department guidelines.

- Shipping can be arranged anywhere in the world.

- A Linwood representative will work with you all the way through the design and construction process.

- Your home package will only contain high quality building materials and is supported by full manufacturer warranty.

- These designs are copyrighted and may not be reproduced in whole or in part without express written permission.

- Photographs and plans may differ slightly due to individual customer preferences. Check with sales representative to confirm construction details.

~ INDEX OF HOMES ~